Tir in s'
wich
LSL
du
£58

844 54

LH218

FROM PISSARRO TO PICASSO
COLOR ETCHING
IN FRANCE

Phillip Dennis Cate
Marianne Grivel

FROM PISSARRO TO PICASSO

COLOR ETCHING

IN FRANCE

Works from the Bibliothèque Nationale
and the Zimmerli Art Museum

Zimmerli Art Museum
Flammarion

This book was published in conjunction with the exhibition
From Pissarro to Picasso: Color Etching in France

**The Jane Voorhees Zimmerli Art Museum,
Rutgers, The State University of New Jersey**
September 27 to November 29, 1992

Vincent Van Gogh Museum, Amsterdam
February 12 to April 18, 1993

Bibliothèque Nationale, Paris
June 5 to 15 September, 1993

This exhibition and publication are supported in part by grants
from the Florence J. Gould Foundation, the National Endowment for the Arts,
and by an indemnity from the Federal Council on the Arts
and the Humanities.

Marianne Grivel's text was translated from the French by Lisa Davidson
Copyediting by Camilla Sandell and Julie Gaskill
Design by Pascale Ogée
Typesetting by PFC, Dole
Photoengraving by Euresys, Lille and Bussière arts graphiques, Paris
Printed by Imprimerie Clerc S.A., Saint-Amand-Montrond
Binding by SIRC, Marigny-le-Châtel

ISBN: 2-08013-538-4
Dépôt légal: September 1992
No. d'édition: 0509
Printed in France

Frontispiece:

Last Poppies

c. 1897

Théodore Roussel

Standing Nude

1906-07

Pablo Picasso

Contents

ACKNOWLEDGEMENTS

The Bibliothèque Nationale's unsurpassed holdings of French turn-of-the-century prints have been a major inspiration and model for the development over the last twenty years of the Zimmerli's concentrated but more modest collection. We are, therefore, honored and indebted to the administration of the Bibliothèque Nationale headed by Emmanuel Le Roy Ladurie and to Laure Beaumont-Maillet, Director of the Département des Estampes et de la Photographie for permitting this instructive collaboration between our two institutions. We are very grateful to Arsène Bonafous-Murat, who clarified problems of technique and of English/French printmaking nomenclature. Jean-Claude Romand of the Sagot-Le Garrec gallery generously made available to us the original inventory cards and catalogues of his great-grandfather, Edmond Sagot, the important *fin-de-siècle* dealer and publisher who played a major role in the color etching movement. We would also like to thank the following at the Département des Estampes et de la Photographie: Claude Bouret, chief curator, Françoise Woimant, chief curator, Anne-Marie Sauvage, curator, and Valdo Bouillard, assistant librarian. Catherine Camboulives, former curator at the Musée de Saint-Denis, Félix Gatier, Bertrand Joly, curator at the National Archives and Monique Sevin, curator at the Jacques Doucet Library, also were most helpful and to them we extend our warmest thanks.

In the United States, Sinclair Hitchings, Keeper of Prints at the Boston Public Library, greatly assisted our research by making available to us the library's comprehensive collection of works by the printer-printmaker Eugène Delâtre. This important archive was donated to the library almost fifty years ago by Delâtre's daughter Zélina Delâtre because of the close professional relationship established between her father and Arthur W. Heintzelman (1890-1965), the mid-twentieth-century Keeper of Prints at the Boston Public Library and one-time apprentice to Delâtre. At the Zimmerli Art Museum this project was aided by Barbara Trelstad, Registrar, Roberto Delgato, Preparator, and Lisa Simpson, Research Assistant. We also extend our thanks to Barbara Stern Shapiro and Sue Welsh Reed, Keepers of Prints at the Museum of Fine Arts, Boston.

Thanks must also go to Ronald de Leeuw, Director, and Stefan van Raay, Deputy Director, of the Van Gogh Museum: with the participation of Amsterdam in the tour, the exhibition will reach a broader European public. Finally we would like to thank Jean-François Barrielle, Suzanne Tise and Delphine Le Cesne at Flammarion for the production of the English and French editions of this publication.

We are most grateful to the Florence J. Gould Foundation, New York, and to the National Endowment for the Arts for recognizing the value of this cooperative venture and for supporting From Pissarro to Picasso: Color Etching in France with a major grant.

Phillip Dennis Cate
Marianne Grivel

FOREWORD

The quarrel between black-and-white etching and color etching is an old story, almost as old as the print itself. It is still current, however, and animates many conversations in today's studios. Subjects are not lacking in this dialogue: in the domain of prints, as in others, there are masterpieces and failures; time, color or black-and-white change nothing of this. Who would not agree with Whistler when he said that black ink on white paper was good enough for Rembrandt, and so it was good enough for him? But how many others would not be content merely with Mary Cassatt's subtle "bricolages"?

The conflict lay elsewhere, however. For example, it existed between the painters who did not consider the print as a means of extending their genius to a greater number of people, and the printmakers who, despite their great technical competence, refused to remain in the background, where the professionals of the paintbrush would have liked to keep them. Thus, Lucas Vosterman was somewhat overcome by hubris when he aspired, in his superb interpretations of Rubens, to engrave his name larger than those of the master. But between these two extremes extended a vast space where painter-etchers as much as etcher-painters could encounter a variety of experiences, and the majority did not deny themselves these experiences, with more or less success.

Nonetheless, another point of contention existed between those for whom color prints were primarily an imitation of drawing or painting and those for whom etching and color mutually invigorated each other, creating something perfectly original and very different from painting. On the one hand, there were the German chiaroscurists who, in the early sixteenth century, wanted to apply the effects of drawings in India ink highlighted with white onto colored paper, and on the other, the fabulous, unsurpassed productions of Hercules Seghers. On the one hand, there were purely reproductive intentions, dependent on fashion and commerce, which resulted in etchings in a crayon or pastel manner; and on the other hand, the research of someone like Jakob Christof Le Blon, whose Luminist and Newtonian preoccupations went beyond the concerns of painting in his epoch, which, intellectually speaking, was well antedated by the discovery of quadricolor.

Tired of color lithographs and academism, the Impressionists and their friends rediscovered the aquatint—a colored aquatint free of hindrances other than those of light—and the Japanese print which, since it was a recent discovery, acted as the stimulus. In forty glorious years, between the war of 1870 and that of 1914, they relearned forgotten lessons, limping behind their distant predecessors. Four decades of trial, experimentation, mistakes sometimes, daring always, four decades of masterpieces!

Obviously, the exhibition organized jointly by the Zimmerli Art Museum and the Bibliothèque Nationale shows only the exceptional proofs culled from their collections, with some loans from two other precious holdings, the Chicago Art Institute and the Musée Picasso, whose curators we have the pleasure of thanking. The title of this exhibition, From Pissarro to Picasso, emphasizes, as can easily be understood, the names of two stars of painting. But these two artists, one at his apogee, the other only beginning, were also indisputably masters of printmaking. And, under this title chosen with taste and intelligence by Phillip Dennis Cate, director of the Zimmerli Art Museum and by Marianne Grivel, former curator at the Département des Estampes et de la Photographie of the Bibliothèque Nationale, some fifty printmakers, often little known to the general public, demonstrate their brilliant and multifaceted talent. Their presence bears evidence to the vitality, forever rejuvenated, of the art of the print.

Emmanuel Le Roy Ladurie
Professor at the Collège de France
General Administrator at the Bibliothèque Nationale

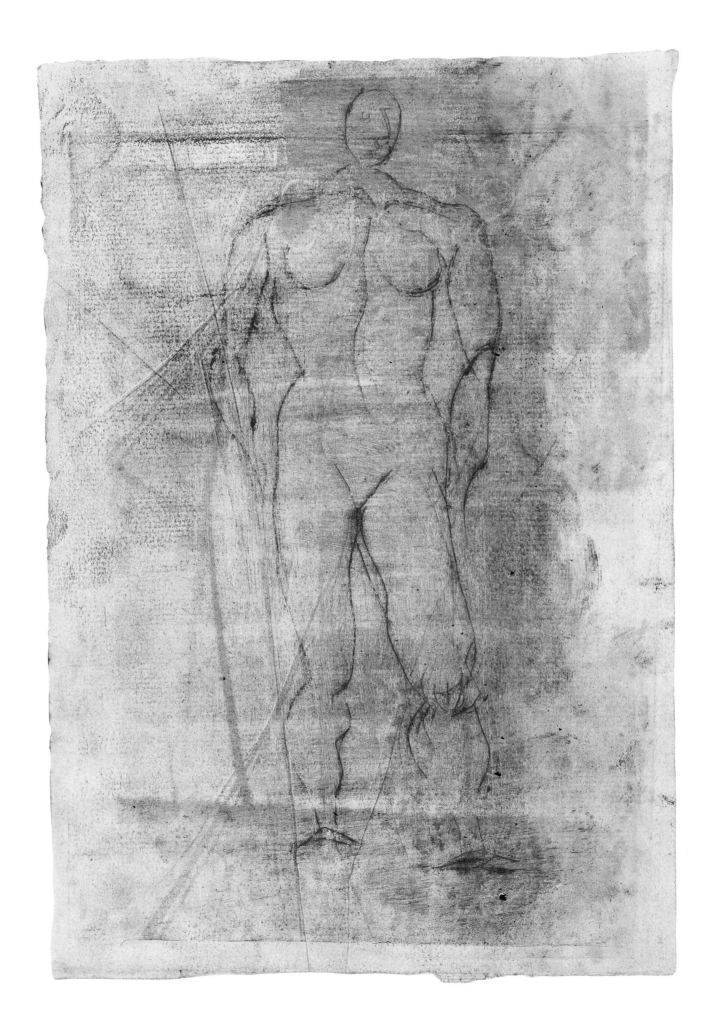

PREFACE

During the summer of 1976, I spent an intensive ten weeks at the Bibliothèque Nationale in Paris investigating *fin-de-siècle* printmaking and photo-printing processes, supported by a grant from the National Endowment for the Arts, a federal agency in Washington, D.C. The extensive collections of the Département des Estampes et de la Photographie, the Département des Imprimés and the Département des Périodiques gave me a much better understanding—both visual and intellectual—of the complicated and varied commercial and artistic printing processes which evolved during the second half of the nineteenth century in France. This enriching experience also allowed me much greater knowledge of the work of many significant but not necessarily well-known painter-printmakers of the period. Two specific exhibitions with related publications resulted from that summer of enlightenment: Printing in France, 1850-1900: The Artist and New Technologies (The Grolier Club, N.Y., Spring 1978) and The Color Revolution: Color Lithography in France, 1890-1900 (The Zimmerli Art Museum, The Baltimore Museum of Art, The Boston Public Library, September 1978-July 1979).

From Pissarro to Picasso: Color Etching in France is, in essence, a sequel to the 1978 Color Revolution exhibition. For the first exhibition, the Zimmerli's fledgling collection of French color lithographs was supplemented by loans from numerous other institutions in the United States. Forty percent of the Color Etching exhibition derives from the Zimmerli collection and almost sixty percent from the extraordinary holdings of the Département des Estampes of the Bibliothèque Nationale. Of the 200 works by fifty artists selected for the exhibition, only Picasso's very rare experiments in color etching had to be borrowed from other collections. We are, therefore, most thankful to Douglas Druick and Suzanne McCullagh at the Chicago Art Institute, Gérard Regnier (now Directeur des Musées de France), and Paule Mazouet and Brigitte Leal at the Musée Picasso for allowing some important early works to be included in this project. Without these loans the title of the exhibition would have been meaningless!

In contrast to lithography, whereby images are printed from a flat or planographic surface, and to woodblock or wood-engraving, whereby images are obtained from relief surfaces, this exhibition focuses upon images obtained from intaglio, that is, incised, surfaces. For purposes of simplification, a certain license has been taken with the generic use of the term "color etching": etching, whereby a metal plate is incised by the action of acid, is but one of three basic intaglio processes which comprise this exhibition. The other two processes, drypoint and engraving, do not involve the application of acid onto plates at all; rather, an incised printing surface is obtained by means of sharp pointed tools cutting directly into the surface of a plate.

Although the art and movements of *fin-de-siècle* color lithography and color relief printing have been explored, codified and exhibited over the last century, little attention has been paid to the particular aesthetic qualities and history of intaglio color printing and its school of artists since Gabriel Mourey's two-part article entitled "Coloured Etchings in France," published in *The Studio* in 1901. The purpose of From Pissarro to Picasso: Color Etching in France, is, therefore, to present for the first time color intaglio printmaking as an active and pervasive artistic movement from about 1890 to 1910 with its own particular history, distinctive aesthetics and leading participants.

Phillip Dennis Cate,
Director, The Jane Voorhees Zimmerli Art Museum

C. P.

mo 1/11

INTRODUCTION

THE ORIGINS AND RENAISSANCE OF COLOR ETCHING

The first experiments with color intaglio printing date from the seventeenth century. Until that time, color had occasionally been added to images by an illuminator who used pattern and stencil, or sometimes brush, to color popular engravings, almanacs and what were widely known as *semi-fine* prints from the rue Saint-Jacques in Paris. L'*Académie de la peinture nouvelle mise au jour pour instruire la jeunesse à bien peindre en huile et en mignature* (1679) by La Fontaine provides specific information on the colors used in the seventeenth century: ivory, coal and lampblacks, Bremen blue and indigo. Yellows were obtained from yellow ochre, yellow lake or Buckthorn lake; vermilion, red ochre, Brazilwood lake, dragon's blood and crimson lake produced various reds; greens were obtained from verdigris, *vert de vessie* and green earth (green was, of course, also obtained by mixing two primary colors, Prussian blue and yellow lake, but the resulting color was not permanent). All these pigments were reasonably priced, with the exception of the markedly more expensive lapis.

From the sixteenth century, engravers began to print their etchings in color. This idea almost certainly came from Italy which, along with Germany, was one of the two centers of monochrome engraving in the early part of the century. We are familiar with the sanguine impressions printed by Domenico Campagnola (1500-64). The practice was probably brought to France by Antonio Fantuzzi, who worked in Fontainebleau in the mid-sixteenth century. Jean Duvet (b. after 1485-d.1561) pulled impressions of Saint Sebastian, Saint Anthony, and Saint Roch, and of the suicide of Judas, printed in red, purple, and brown ink.

In the seventeenth century during the reign of Louis XIII, prints made with colored inks were produced by François Perrier (1590-1660) and especially by Abraham Bosse (1602-76). The Bibliothèque Nationale and the Archives Nationales house letter patents dated January 6, 1637 which "allow Mr. Abraham Bosse, intaglio engraver, and Mr. Charles Delafont to print on all materials of silk, paper, vellum, parchment, copper, etc., using leather, etching, wood or other, with all the colors used by oil painters and illuminators to imitate all kinds of colors, from flesh tones to tints, colored according to the pigments, and embellished with borders and gold or silver adornments using engraving or etching methods." This privilege protected their invention for five years, under penalty of confiscation of any counterfeit work and a fine of 1,500 pounds.[1]

139

Church and Farm at Éragny, 1894

Camille Pissarro

In 1971 Hyatt Mayor wrote that Bosse definitely used this technique to print the fans that he manufactured and sold in the Galerie du Palais. Sue Welsh Reed, curator of the Museum of Fine Arts in Boston, recently demonstrated that some of Bosse's engravings in the Print Department of the Bibliothèque Nationale were overprinted with white.[2]

There are other seventeenth-century color engravings in existence. In *Étude sur les livres à figures édités en France de 1601 à 1660*,[3] Jeanne Duportal writes of two books illustrated with prints of this kind: *Peristromata turcica, sive dissertatio emblematica, praesentem Europae Stratum ingeniosis coloribus representans*, an anonymous work published in 1640 by Toussaint du Bray, includes etched figures printed in red and black; a more sophisticated work, *Le Maréchal de Bataille* by Lostelneau, published by Migon in 1647, is illustrated with etched, engraved, wood, and relief prints produced in yellow, red, and black.

Color etching therefore existed long before the inventions of Jakob Christof Le Blon (1670-1741), an engraver from Frankfurt who worked in England and in France, and who is generally attributed with the invention of color printing using registered plates. He based his techniques on Newton's theories and superimposed the three primary colors over a mezzotint.

Portrait of Louis XV, after a painting by Nicholas Blakey, was printed in 1739 using mezzotint and aquatint and the superimposition of four color plates; it is an exceptional example of the process for which Le Blon had obtained a royal patent. Jacques-Fabien Gautier-Dagoty (1716-85) and his four sons adopted this technique that Le Blon claimed to have invented, creating anatomical and botanical plates, portraits, and genre pieces which, once glued to canvas and varnished, looked almost like paintings.

Engravings in the crayon manner—employed by Jean-Charles François (1717-69) and Gilles Demarteau (1722-76)—and aquatint, developed by Jean-Baptiste Le Prince (1734-81), remained fashionable throughout the reign of Louis XV, who considered that prints were an excellent way to decorate apartments. While wealthy collectors could purchase drawings by Boucher or Baudouin, color reproductions of their work were accessible to a much larger public. This explains the success of artist Louis-Marin Bonnet, "the only pastel engraver," who specialized in portraits of women in the style of Boucher; the most beautiful example of his work is *Portrait of Flore*, printed from eight color plates.

Some of these artists also used a technique that was simpler than the process of registering several plates: etching *à la poupée*, used around 1765 by Bartolozzi in London. As opposed to multiplate color etching, which required as many plates as there were colors—or at least the use of four plates corresponding to the three primary colors, red, yellow, and blue, plus black—this technique required only a single run through the press. Thus, in the late eighteenth century, Jean-François Janinet (1752-1814), Charles Melchior Descourtis (1753-1820) and Philibert Louis Debucourt (1755-1832) were able to reproduce the delicacy and transparency of watercolors.

After a long eclipse throughout the nineteenth century, the first attempts to revive color etching techniques came in the 1870s; however their actual renaissance did not take place until the 1890s. Unlike color lithography, color etching did not receive immediate acceptance: the former was a mass phenomenon—due largely to poster art—while the latter long remained the preserve of a select public of demanding collectors. The first experiments were the work of isolated artists: Félix Bracquemond and Félix Buhot were followed by Mary Cassatt and Camille Pissarro.

The increasing interest in eighteenth-century etching, a style considered graceful and elegant, was linked to the revival in color etching. The crusade led by the Goncourt brothers, whose collection was sold by the Hôtel Drouot on August 26, 27 and 28, 1897, was evidence of this newfound taste for color. L'*Estampe et l'Affiche*, published by Clément-Janin and Mellerio, specialized in contemporary prints but also demonstrated an interest in eighteenth-century color etchings, noting, for example, the record price obtained at a public sale in Amsterdam for *The Two Kisses*, a color etching by Debucourt dated 1756, which sold for the astronomical sum of 13,750 francs.

The introduction of Japanese prints to France in the 1860s and the Impressionists' passion for color also contributed to an increasing interest in color etching. Letters from Vincent Van Gogh to his brother Théo reveal the fundamental importance of color to artists of this period.

Other important events were the 1867 Universal Exposition; Philippe Burty's articles on Japonisme in L*a Renaissance littéraire et artistique* (1872-73); Théodore Duret's work in *La Gazette des beaux-arts* in 1882; the 1883 retrospective exhibition of Japanese art in the Georges Petit gallery, organized by Louis Gonse, author of L'*Art Japonais*; *Le Japon artistique* published by Siegfried Bing (May 1888 to April 1891), all of which had a considerable impact on color etching.[4] Mary Cassatt, in particular, was strongly influenced by the exhibition of Japanese prints organized by Bing at the École des Beaux-Arts, April 25 to May 22, 1890.

Some of the most passionate supporters of this Japanese art were often the etchers and collectors themselves: among the first members of the Société des Études Japonaises, founded in 1873 by Léon de Rosny, was Henry Sommier, better known as Somm. At the Universal Exhibition of 1867, Félix Bracquemond showed a china table service decorated with a pattern of plants and animals inspired by Hokusai and Hiroshige, commissioned by Eugène Rousseau. Furthermore, publications devoted to Japanese art provided the opportunity to publish color illustration: chromolithographs illustrate both *Sketches of Japanese Manners and Customs* (1867), published by J. M. W. Silver, and volume II of L'*Art* (1875). In 1883, Plon published *Okama*, a Japanese novel with color photo relief illustrations by Félix Regamey. That same

41

Under the Horse Chesnut, 1896-97
Mary Cassatt

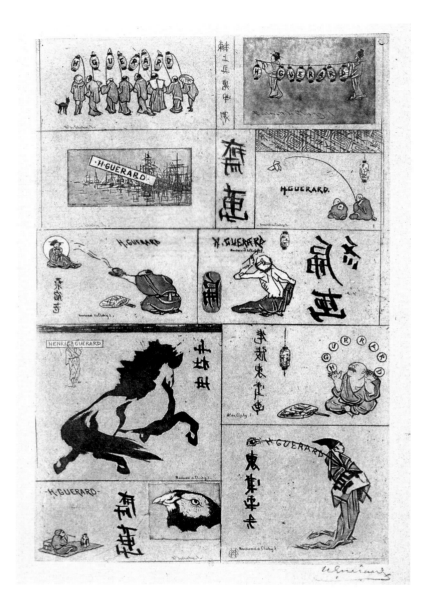

year, Félix Buhot published the album, *Japonisme, Ten Etchings,* which included plates made after 1875 of the Japanese objects in the Philippe Burty collection; the frontispiece by Guérard is sometimes printed in red ink.

Critics and dealers also demonstrated this dual interest in Japan and color etching. Durand-Ruel exhibited paintings, pastels, and engravings by Mary Cassatt in April 1891, and in January and February of 1893, organized an exhibition of prints by Utamaro and Hiroshige. *The Studio* published an article by M. Hill-Burton, "Photography and Color Printing in Japan" (1898, volume XIV), which was followed by Gabriel Mourey's "Colored Etchings in France" (February 1901, volume XXII).

Edmond de Goncourt confirmed this connection between eighteenth-century engraving, Japan, the Impressionists, and color etching. Although highly critical of Mary Cassatt's first exhibition of etchings, he was more indulgent when she showed her color

prints at the Durand-Ruel gallery, November 27 to December 16, 1893: "Saturday, December 2, exhibition by Miss Cassatt. Attempts at coloring plates in the manner of Japanese prints; interesting attempts, but still highly incomplete."[5] "Attempts" is the right word: these first artists working with color etching were experimenting; they did not intend to create lasting works, at least not for the time being. They printed their own plates, and the editions were extremely limited, or even unique.

Félix Bracquemond (1833-1914) provides the best example: he etched and printed his plates at the shop of the printer Auguste Delâtre. By 1856 he had his own press and could pull his own trial proofs. He was an active participant in the Société des Aquafortistes from 1862 to 1867, he was passionately interested in Japanese prints and in color, and in 1885 he published Du Dessin et de la couleur. In 1873, he created Au Jardin d'Acclimatation, an aquatint and etching printed from four plates using the Debucourt technique. The first plate was destroyed, and only six prints were pulled from the second. He did not work with color again until 1893.

Félix Buhot (1847-98) also worked with color printing very early on and produced The National Holiday in 1878. He also pulled his own trial proofs, although he sometimes called on Delâtre or Léon Leroy, the printer for Cadart.

Camille Pissarro (1830-1903) met Edgar Degas in 1878. He began to make monotypes under the influence of Degas, who had mastered the technique and described it as "drawings printed with thick, greasy ink." Dusk with Haystacks was a result of this collaboration between the two artists; various inkings of the monotype are known, indicating a considerable interest in the effects of color. Barbara Stern Shapiro and Michel Melot estimate that there are sixteen monotypes from this period.[6] But on December 23, 1880, Pissarro wrote that "as for etching, I have had neither the time nor the means to continue the experiments; I would have needed two or three years of intense work, we stopped suddenly."[7] More than ten years passed before he worked in color again.

During this same year, 1880, the printer Auguste Delâtre, trained by Charles Jacque, made several color monotypes. Delâtre began to work in 1844 and obtained a license for intaglio printing in Paris on July 8, 1852, which he renewed on December 19, 1857.[8] He printed three monotypes, Effects of Moonlight, in the period from 1880 to 1883, and the results were very similar to the monotypes made by Adolphe Appian from 1863, also printed by Delâtre, and to Count Lepic's "mobile etchings." Delâtre's technique, in fact, involved nothing more than inking the plate in an area already laid out with drypoint and roulette.

Working at the same time as Degas, Henri-Charles Guérard (1846-77) also excelled in the monotype technique and contributed to its revival. In Paris à l'eau-forte (October 4, 1874), he explained his "etching with silk," which produced such successful inking effects that he received letters from New York and Boston requesting advice. Attracted by color, he would readily add areas of gouache or paint to his etchings (The Three Philosophers). The Bibliothèque Nationale's title proof of Japonisme, Ten Etchings is somewhat clumsy: the copper plate was varnished incorrectly, and acid leaked under the varnish, resulting in an appearance of false biting. Around 1885, he tried color etching using several registered copper plates. He printed his own works, varied the editions, replaced blue ink with bistre, endlessly elaborating his experiments. In the Garden demonstrates the intensity of this inventive artist, who obtained "a particular pleasure in differenti-

54
Night,
c. 1883
Auguste Delâtre

53
Landscape,
c. 1880
Auguste Delâtre

ating the effects of his proofs." Annotations reveal the artist's exacting approach: "A single print from the only red plate before the two flowerpots on the left and the one at the bottom of the dress"; "modeled background, clear sky, leaves in the sky before the two flowerpots on the left and the one at the bottom of the dress—state of the yellow plate. Single impression"; "print the blue."

Thus the first isolated attempts at etching in color during the years 1870-80 were succeeded by a more marked interest in the technique. Two Impressionist painters in particular were at the forefront of the movement: Mary Cassatt and Camille Pissarro. Yet when Gabriel Mourey examined the phenomenon of etching (*The Studio*, February 1901), he cited as precursors Raffaëlli, Bracquemond (misspelled "Bracquemand" in the article), Legrand, Eugène Delâtre, Houdard, Lepère, Ranft and, above all, Charles Maurin, "for to him, I believe, the honor exclusively belongs," omitting Cassatt and Pissarro.[9] In 1913, Raffaëlli proposed another more complete list, including Cassatt, Bracquemond, Guérard, Marie Gautier, Maurin, Rops, Gaujan, Eugène Delâtre, and himself, adding, justly, that "posterity will judge which among us did the most to advance this movement

86

In the Garden,
before 1886
Henri Guérard
Right-hand page: final state. Left-hand
page, from top to bottom and from right
to left: 1st state of the yellow plate,
2nd state of the red plate, proof resulting
from the combination of red and yellow
plates, 3rd state of the blue plate,
4th state of the blue plate and pulled
with the yellow, proof resulting from the
combination of blue and yellow plates,
proof of the black plate.

72

Child in the Park,
c. 1900

Eugène Delâtre

which is of great artistic interest. . . . Yes, this dispute is futile, because I believe that any etcher worthy of the name must have made, during his life, some attempt at color etching."[10] In fact, Renoir made a color etching and drypoint, *Mother and Child*, for Vollard's *L'Album des Peintres-Graveurs* in 1896; that same year, Edvard Munch used drypoint and aquatint on zinc for *Young Woman by the Water*; and in 1905-06, Francis Picabia made four color etchings, *Sunset on Port-de-Bouc*, *Return from Fishing (Les Martigues)*, *The Bridge at Villeneuve-sur-Yonne (Effects of Snow)* and *Banks of the Loing at Montigny (Effects of Fog)*.

120b

Montmartre with View of Paris, c. 1900

Charles Maurin

FROM PISSARRO TO PICASSO:
THE REVIVAL OF COLOR ETCHING
IN FRANCE

1873-91: EARLY EXPERIMENTS IN COLOR ETCHING

The generations of Pissarro and Picasso represent, respectively, the beginning and the end of the initial movement in artistic color etching. For our purposes this movement is confined to the period of approximately twenty years from 1890 through the first decade of the twentieth century. Until the 1890s "original" artistic printmaking was generally accepted as a black-and-white medium. Color was reserved for "reproductive" prints copying works in other media such as painting or drawing and for publications not normally considered artistic, such as hand-colored Épinal folk prints and popular, stencil-colored, illustrated journals that by the early 1880s had become highly industrialized, their images produced by partly photomechanical color-relief printing processes. In the 1870s and 1880s color lithography, until then primarily an industrial printing process, was just coming into its own as an artistic medium, thanks principally to the efforts of poster artist Jules Chéret; yet color lithography was not entirely accepted as an artistic process until the 1890s, when many artists demonstrated that its great aesthetic potential as a printmaking medium extended far beyond commercial or advertisement purposes.[1] Only then did preconceived notions about the hierarchy within color printmaking permit the artistic development of color etching.

While Félix Bracquemond's Au Jardin d'Acclimatation of 1873 is the first known attempt by a nineteenth-century French artist to create a print in more than one color from several intaglio plates, it was an isolated example that did not attract the immediate interest of other artists. In fact, Bracquemond himself did not work in the medium again for at least twenty years. Meanwhile, Henri Guérard, a friend and colleague of Bracquemond and Degas, experimented more actively with color etching as early as 1868 when he printed in the single color blue, à la poupée, Manet's Boy Blowing Bubble.[2] Ten years later, Degas would achieve the same kind of effect with Pissarro's Dusk with Haystacks by printing proofs either in blue or, as in the case of the impression at the Bibliothèque Nationale, "Van Dyck brown." In 1878, Guérard's close friend, Félix Buhot, who was a prolific etcher, created The National Holiday in which the narrative borders of various impressions were colored à la poupée, in gold or red. More than one impression was printed from a single plate in red, blue, yellow, and black.

Henri Guérard, Félix Buhot, and the young Henri Rivière experimented often with printing one color other than black during the early 1880s. Some of Rivière's earliest attempts at printmaking, such as his two dramatic seascapes, were inspired by Buhot's use of blue in the The Small Funeral of 1883. Buhot's compositional devices, rather than his colors, inspired one of Rivière's prints depicting figures scurrying under umbrellas in the rain.[3]

For a special dinner organized in 1883 by the publisher Dentu, Guérard printed an etched menu in red. That same year, he designed the frontispiece for Buhot's album Japonisme, Ten Etchings, of which the Bibliothèque Nationale's impression is printed in red. Guérard's fascination with color printing during

27

The National
Holiday of 30th June
on boulevard Clichy,
1878
Félix Buhot

21
*Au Jardin
d'Acclimatation,*
1873
Félix Bracquemond
(Detail on
facing page)

the 1880s led him to explore a variety of techniques including printing in one color (red or blue), *à la poupée*, and *au repérage*. He even developed an unusual and highly innovative technique for *Twenty Grotesque Masks*: he cut down each plate into the shape of the drypoint-designed mask, inked the intaglio lines of the masks to delineate the eyes, nose, mouth, et cetera in black, and inked the surface of the masks in color *à la poupée*. He then placed several masks together on the press and printed them simultaneously on one sheet of paper.

The dating of Guérard's prints is often imprecise; to add to the problem, it is known that he printed impressions from the same plate over the years. His plates for *Masks*, for example, were first printed around 1875 and were used over and over again in a variety of ways for the next twenty years. When Guérard's prints are not specifically dated in the plate or on the paper, the

137

*Dusk with
Haystacks,*
1879
Camille Pissarro

28

The Small Funeral,
1883
Félix Buhot

160

*House on the Edge
of the Water,*
1884
Henri Rivière

159

Les Ébihiens,
1884
Henri Rivière

only means of approximating the earliest year for their execution is the catalogue for his exhibition held at the Bernheim-Jeune gallery from December 1887 through January 1888. The show included a number of prints in one or more colors, but as Bertin pointed out, it is obvious that many were produced before 1887.[4] Among them is Guérard's *Punchinello*, printed in red, blue, and yellow from three separate plates. Bertin suggests that Guérard's first efforts to create color prints by the superimposition of plates occurred as early as 1885: *In the Garden*, based on Guérard's painting by the same name, was exhibited in the 1886 Salon, but may easily have been the product of the previous year's work.[5]

By 1890 Guérard was considered the master of color etching. The fact that the technique was finally recognized as appropriate for artistic printmaking, if only in avant-garde circles, was made clear by Octave Uzanne's praise of Guérard in an article written in 1890 for the literary review *Le Livre moderne*.[6] Guérard's *Punchinello* and proofs of its red, yellow, and blue plates illustrated the article to demonstrate the three-color printing process.

"Guérard has already tried his hand at this with varying degrees of success. He is at the forefront of those who, through the originality of their knowledge and the special genius of the painter-etcher, may soon herald a new era of contemporary printmaking."[7]

Other than Guérard, Buhot and Rivière, Jean-François Raffaëlli and Henry-Julien Detouche were the other major artists prior to 1890 to experiment, albeit on a very limited basis, with color printmaking using the *à la poupée* system. In 1882 and 1884 Raffaëlli produced several trial color proofs of different images in this manner;[8] these were followed in 1886 by Detouche's three-color *At the Theater*.

One of the most important influences on the early development of the color etching movement came from a series of images of Punchi-

Above:

Henri Boutet

Punchinello,
1889
Etching
Zimmerli Art
Museum, Mindy
and Ramon
Tublitz Purchase
Fund

Below:

Édouard Manet

Punchinello,
1874
Color lithograph
Zimmerli Art
Museum, Friends
Purchase Fund

nello produced by Henri Boutet and Henri Guérard. In 1889 Boutet's humorous rendition of *Punchinello* was included in the second of a series of albums published by the Société de l'Estampe Originale. Boutet had originally created this etching for the 1884 Exposition des Arts Incohérents, where it was photomechanically reproduced in the exhibition's satirical catalogue and annotated with the following text: "Pan! Pan! What is this? It's the striking portrait of our future President of the Council of Ministers. . . ."[9] Boutet's choice of subject clearly referred to Manet's notorious 1874 color lithograph, *Punchinello*, which had been censored on publication by the new conservative Republican government because of the likeness of the pompous old buffoon to President MacMahon. Manet's print was controversial not only politically, but also artistically, because it appeared at a time when no artists (except for poster artists such as Jules Chéret) used the commercial process of color lithography for an original work that was not intended for magazine or newspaper illustration. Although Boutet's first *Punchinello* was printed only in black and white, when he included the etching, now without text, in the 1889 L'*Estampe originale* album, he hand-colored the paper with yellow, green and rust pigment to simulate a color etching. Surprisingly, it was the only color print in any medium found within this publication that professed to promote up-to-date aesthetic concerns in printmaking. As such, it is interesting that the image of *Punchinello* in the tradition of Manet became the battle cry for early efforts in color etching, real or simulated, at a time when the established art community frowned upon any form of original print in color.

Guérard's version of *Punchinello* was also probably a homage to his friend Manet, who died in 1883. Guérard's reference to Manet gives the work a new dimension that links it to political commentary by artists or, at the very least, to political allusions within the artistic community. Guérard's decision to print his *Punchinello* in color, therefore, was yet another means by which he alluded to and paralleled the radical nature of Manet's print.

Guérard, Buhot, and Rivière each created important work in one color. Although they were preceded in this technique by Camille Pissarro, for whom monochromatic printing (in red or blue) was certainly a direct way to suggest the changing effects of light on a landscape at different times of day in the Impressionist manner, their one-color prints were clearly derived from the art of Japan.[10] Among the most astute observers of Japanese art at the end of the last century, these three artists not only imitated the subjects, styles of depiction, and bold compositional elements of Japanese prints, and specifically the *ukiyo-e* prints of Hokusai and Hiroshige, but they also sought to replicate the same inks and paper.[11] Their knowledge of Japanese art allowed them to anticipate the theory that "less is more"; when they each stamped their Japanese-inspired red monogram on their blue etchings, the results were often quite dramatic, emphasizing the strength of unmixed colors in the suggestion of mood. The precedent for and the function of monochromatic color etching were, therefore, well established in the 1880s, and there was to be a continuous line of such work by many artists for more than a decade, though not necessarily inspired directly by Japan, culminating in Picasso's *The Frugal Repast* in blue of 1904 and his two versions of *Standing Nude* in red of 1906-07. *The Frugal Repast* was Picasso's second attempt at printmaking, and his first print made in France. The two known impressions printed in blue or blue-green by Eugène Delâtre represent a conscious effort on the part of the artist to express the angst of his Blue Period in a medium he was just learning to master.[12] Not since Pissarro's *Dusk with Haystacks* had monochromatic blue etching had such an intense relationship with an artist's purpose.

BREAKING THE COLOR BARRIER

The Impressionists tried to apply their interest in capturing the effects of light and color on varied surfaces to the printmaking medium. In 1879, when Degas printed Pissarro's *Dusk with Haystacks* in monochromatic blue or red, he was

Picasso

planning to publish a journal of prints that would feature etchings by Pissarro, Raffaëlli, Cassatt, Bracquemond, and himself. It was to be entitled *Le Jour et la Nuit*, and although its images were to be primarily in black and white, Degas gave some consideration to producing works in color by means of woodblocks or stencils, or by color printing on top of simple etchings or softground images.[13] Coincidentally, in that same year Bracquemond's color etching *Au Jardin d'Acclimatation* of 1873 was included in the fourth Impressionist exhibition, yet, despite the basic coloristic concerns of the Impressionists, neither this etching nor the color options for *Le Jour et la Nuit* inspired attempts in color etching by Degas or his colleagues, although they were all vigorously and innovatively exploring black-and-white intaglio techniques. The journal was never published, and while Degas's printmaking *œuvre* includes various examples of monotypes colored over in pastel, unlike Pissarro, Bracquemond, Raffaëlli, and Cassatt, he has no color etchings to his credit.

In effect, by the end of the 1880s, black-and-white etching remained the preferred printmaking technique for most artists. In his study on etching, the American graphic artist and illustrator Joseph Pennell remarked: "Etchings and other intaglio plates may be printed in color in many ways—have been for years—one only worse than the other." James McNeill Whistler once said that black ink on white paper was good enough for Rembrandt, and so it was good enough for him.[14]

In spite of this preference for black-and-white etching, there was evidence of a burgeoning interest in color printmaking by the beginning of the 1890s. In an article entitled "La Gravure en couleurs," Baron Roger Portalis questioned the suitability of color etching as a printmaking medium:

"Etching in black, with needle and acid, remains for us, as indeed it should remain for everyone, the only genuine etching; but it must be admitted that the ingenious processes of color etching are of some interest. They have added spice to our libraries and to our portfolios. . . . How will color etching develop in the future? Will it fall for good into the domain of industry or will it be rescued by the hands of true artists? We have high hopes for its future, but we do not have the gift of foresight, and regret that we are not able to answer the intriguing question: what will become of color etching?"[15]

The art establishment, however, was not as generous as Portalis. In 1891, as printmakers in all media were beginning to break the color barrier, the Société des Artistes Français passed a ruling that disallowed any color prints in its annual Salon; this regulation existed until 1899.[16] In 1898, the *Journal des Artistes* recorded the debates generated by the success of color etching. Henri Lefort, a mediocre artist, but president of the lithography and etching section of the Société des Artistes Français, considered that "the art of etching is unquestionably the art of 'black and white,'" and was opposed to exhibiting color etchings in the Salon. Charles Maurin, who had just made two series of eight color drypoints, *Sentimental Education* and *Little Class* (1897) printed by Gustave Pellet, and had included two etchings, *Nude Women* and *Eve*, in two albums devoted to the Peintres Graveurs, published in 1897 and 1898 by the Vollard gallery, replied to Lefort on March 20, 1898. He protested "against M. Lefort's pretensions" in the name of "the many etchers who, for ten years, have given a new energy to original French printing, an art that Mr. President denigrates with the childish and contemptuous label of 'the colored image.'" This indignant reply was necessary in the face of continuing opposition. In *L'Estampe et l'Affiche* (April 1897), a magazine considered to be favorable to color etching, Loÿs Delteil wrote that "the art of etching has deviated significantly over the years from the fundamental principles that govern it. In other words, it is no longer sufficient that it remain what it should always be: a black-and-white drawing on white paper. Part of its interest has been drawn from the painter's palette or the sculptor's relief—as it was earlier in the eighteenth century. In other words, color etching is attempting to reproduce the appearance of a pastel or watercolor, an embossed or color

relief. Can etching gain anything from this development? I don't think so. It will certainly attract curiosity, but this dominant aspect will inevitably lower it to the status of an insipid art that exists because of technical compromises and superficial imitations. I must admit that I cannot understand a painting that imitates a print, and vice versa."[17] In *Voltaire* (March 30, 1898), Roger Marx replied to Thiébaut-Sisson's article in *Le Temps* by writing a vibrant defense of color etching. "The contemporary school now includes too many eminent colorists for them to be judged fairly in their absence; furthermore, this ostracism directly contradicts the long-stated preferences of historians and collectors. . . . Work by master artists teaches us that in the past, wood, stone, and metal have always been used for multicolor inking; no incompatibility exists between the material and the process." In 1913 Raffaëlli wrote, "Some people—who failed to notice the names of the great artists that we had among us—would have had us believe that all these etchings exhibited were photoengravings or whimsical works unworthy of the art."[18]

However, Portalis did not have to wait long for a response to his question. By 1891, almost concurrently, four artists had begun to experiment with printing from more than one plate to create color etchings that no longer relied upon the inconsistent touches of the *à la poupée* method. Their greatest obstacle was the difficult and tedious task of accurately superimposing one inked plate after another onto the single piece of paper which would carry the final, multicolor image. As Jules Adeline explained in 1894:

"One of the great problems in printing is the *repérage*: the impressions should fall exactly upon one another, but when printing on damp paper this is not always easy to achieve. By using special marks or, if the margins of the proofs are wide enough, by drawing corners or lines on a sheet of zinc matching the copper plate—it is advisable that all the plates should be of the same dimensions—one can, by carefully placing the sheets of paper on these marked plates and matching each corner of the paper with the corners drawn on the zinc, one can, in this way, print each plate with certainty.

Jean-François Raffaëlli
Les Types de Paris,
published by
Le Figaro,
1889
Zimmerli Art
Museum, Herbert
D. and Ruth
Schimmel
Library Fund

All the same, one must account for variations in pressure and the inevitable stretching of the damp paper as it passes under the roller. All these difficulties, as well as unexpected ones, make the process of intaglio printing with several plates long and expensive.

"In some cases, moreover, registration marks are made not in the margin, but in the actual subject. One should select two areas at the top and the base of the composition on the main axis of the plate, if possible inked in a dark or neutral tone and preferably not too eyecatching. Small perforations in these two places will assure the exact superposition of the paper during the printing of various plates and, once the printing is finished, these little holes—admittedly, they are undesirable—may be filled by carefully pressing down the paper; however, registration marks are indispensable for printing in color."[19]

Bracquemond and Guérard, supposedly, had worked out their own means of duplicating the eighteenth-century system of printing *au repérage*; however, there were no printing ateliers that offered this expertise to less technically adept artists. In 1889 Raffaëlli began to

147

The Actress,
1898
**Jean-François
Raffaëlli**

145

The Seine at Asnières, 1893

Jean-François Raffaëlli

27

The National Holiday of 30th June on boulevard Clichy (detail), 1878

Félix Buhot

experiment with printing in color from several plates, but was not satisfied with the results and could not find a printer to assist him.[20] The following year at his country home in Éragny, Camille Pissarro, with the aid of his son Lucien, began to explore Debucourt's traditional method of printing from four plates—red, yellow, blue, plus black. Yet their frustrations with the process delayed any further efforts until 1894, when the elder Pissarro acquired a printing press from the studio of Auguste and Eugène Delâtre.[21] Mary Cassatt experimented with printing in color, *à la poupée*, with one impression of each of her three mother and child softground and aquatint prints of 1889-90.[22] She employed Marcellin Desboutin's printer, Leroy, to collaborate on her important series of ten color etchings in 1890-91.[23] Charles Maurin experimented with color printing in the beginning of the decade, and by December 1891 he had registered a patent for a hybrid process somewhere between lithography and monotype. Yet he soon

rejected this watercolor-like process for a basic three-color intaglio system with which he had already experimented to some extent.[24]

While Guérard may be the "father" of the color etching movement (one must consider Bracquemond's 1873 color etching as seminal, but without great consequence), Raffaëlli, Pissarro, Maurin, and Cassatt were the real pioneers. The question of who among these four artists was the first to print color etchings from more than one plate is probably impossible to answer. What is significant is that they were all attempting, almost simultaneously, to rediscover multiplate color etching, but each was striving for different visual effects. Of the four, Pissarro was the least influential; his color etchings were limited to small editions (under ten), and were quite personal investigations. Only later, in the early decades of the twentieth century, did posthumous printings make them available to a wide audience; yet, as Barbara Stern Shapiro has pointed out, these later

*Woman with
a Parasol,*
c. 1895
Eugène Delâtre

prints lack much of the spontaneity and richness of the early impressions.[25]

The young printer Eugène Delâtre played a very important early and sustained role as technician and instructor. He was also a prolific producer of his own color etchings, a number of which are artistically significant within the entire spectrum of the movement.

Around 1890 artists became interested in creating color etchings for several reasons. The

1889 and 1890 exhibitions of the Société des Peintres-Graveurs in which Cassatt and Pissarro participated included examples of the multiple-plate medium by Guérard, while the 1889 exhibition also included Buhot's red, yellow, blue, and black trial proof, *à la poupée*, of his 1878 *The National Holiday.*[26] These isolated experiments, however, were not enough to stimulate the relative burst of color etching activity. Other influences included those that encouraged the great contemporaneous flourishing of color lithography: the appealing color lithographic posters of Jules Chéret, the development of photomechanical color printing processes in the 1880s and their use to illustrate popular journals and books, and the continued interest in and greater availability of Japanese color woodblock prints.[27]

The Arts and Crafts Movement played a strong role in the proliferation of artistic color lithography in the 1890s. Although it did not directly influence activities in color etching, it did create an intellectual climate supportive of the relationship between artists and craftsmen and a general wave of enthusiasm for color printing.[28] By the end of the 1890s, when color etching had become technically feasible for many artists, essentially due to the counsel of Eugène Delâtre, it became an alternative to color lithography for those artists seeking either a new aesthetic printmaking experience or a less mass-oriented medium.

It is significant that in 1893 the commercial printing and publishing firm of Boussod, Valadon & Company sponsored two exhibitions at its main office gallery on the boulevard des Capucines. One featured the firm's new publication of six color etchings by Raffaëlli entitled *Types of Simple Folk;*[29] the other was an exhibition of the work of Charles Maurin and his close friend Henri de Toulouse-Lautrec.[30] It was certainly in the interest of Boussod, Valadon & Company to promote the endeavors of artists working in color printmaking. In the 1880s and 1890s, this company had used the coloristic talents of artists, including Toulouse-Lautrec, to illustrate its journal *Le Figaro illustré* and the 1889 serial publication *Les Types de Paris*. Using the relatively new photorelief color printing process (chromophotogravure) invented by Charles Gillot in the early 1880s, Raffaëlli also created wonderful double-page illustrations depicting a traveling circus, dancers at a café-concert, and Parisian genre scenes for *Le Paris illustré*.[31] The ten installments of *Les Types de Paris* featured stories by realist and symbolist writers such as Émile Zola, Guy de Maupassant, J. K. Huysmans, and Stéphane Mallarmé, each illustrated by Raffaëlli with black-and-white and stencil-colored images along with the Gillot photorelief printing system for red, gold, and blue.

Raffaëlli's predilection for linear rather than tonal designs and his use of subtle touches of color worked perfectly with stenciled colors and the relief printing process, which could render only black-and-white contrast (unlike photoengraving, which reproduced the full tonal range of paintings). The plates for photorelief illustrations were made by placing a photographic glass negative of a line drawing over a zinc plate covered with a photosensitive emulsion and then exposing this combination to light. The black or opaque areas of the negative protected the emulsion, while the white or transparent areas of the glass negative allowed light to harden the exposed emulsion that corresponded, in effect, to the original drawing's black lines. Once the unhardened emulsion was washed off the plate by water, the plate was immersed in an acid bath; the acid ate away the surface of the plate unprotected by the hard emulsion and thus left the lines of the initial drawing in relief, ready to be printed. Black-and-white proofs were taken from this relief plate and colored by the artist. These proofs served as the models for the technicians who then produced manually and non-photographically the relief plates for each color.[32]

Raffaëlli's experience during the 1880s in making illustrations colored by relief plates or by stencil for commercial publications inspired him to experiment with similar aesthetic effects in the traditional media of etching and drypoint. There is no exact record of Raffaëlli's 1889 attempts at color etching; one might assume that they relate to his 1893 *Types of Simple Folk* series, which combined subtle intaglio processes. In

1898 Georges Lecomte discussed Raffaëlli's technique in an article for *L'Estampe et l'Affiche*: "How does M. Raffaëlli work? He has no system and no bias. His feelings dictate the way in which he works each plate. Instinctively, he adopts the method which best suits his design."[33] Lecomte then described in great detail how in one print, *Les Invalides*[34] of 1894, the artist created five plates to produce the most subtle color effects:

64b

Woman with a Parasol, c. 1895 **Eugène Delâtre**

"The blue of the sky is portrayed by a smudge of sulfur which bites into the copper, the bodice of a woman in the foreground by two or three strokes of the needle, and this first plate is inked with blue. A second plate, worked with the needle, will provide the red of a flag, some epaulettes and a few branches of trees. The yellow dome of Les Invalides will be inked onto a third plate. On the fourth plate a slight grain with resin will bite out the metal enough for the helmets of the soldiers to be tinted in gray-blue. The fifth plate will be the black one, to be printed over all the rest and to outline strongly the already recognizable shape of these patches of color."[35]

Finally, Lecomte described the simplicity of Raffaëlli's most recent work, which included *The Actress*: "Three, four or five plates are scratched solely with drypoint, without any acid, without the slightest grain. Lines of color, alone, interwoven like an embroidery, give the impression of a drawing that, at the same time, is all color!"[36]

Indeed, Raffaëlli's works employ such minimal color that one wonders why he went to the trouble of creating a sequence of plates for each image. They are more akin to simple but elegant etchings or drypoint prints, highlighted in color *à la poupée* or with watercolor applied by hand or by stencil onto the paper. They are the extreme opposite of the work of most of Raffaëlli's contemporaries, who relied heavily on the textures and grains produced by softground etching and aquatint, sulfur, and pure acid bites. If Raffaëlli's use of color in his work did not make a major impact on color etching, his enthusiasm for the medium and his efforts to organize La Société de la Gravure Originale en Couleur did much to advance the color etching movement. This society began to take form after Raphaëlli's exhibition of color prints at Siegfreid Bing's Art Nouveau gallery in 1898, and finally came to fruition in 1904 under his presidency, when the Georges Petit gallery agreed to hold the group's first Salon.

THE INFLUENCE OF JAPAN

When Félix Buhot produced his 1883 series, *Japonisme, Ten Etchings*, his goal was not so much to duplicate Japanese methods as to document Japanese objects from the Philippe Burty collection (although he did evoke certain qualities of Japanese aesthetics by varying his papers and inks from album to album).[37] When, in 1889, Rivière decided to investigate the Japanese method, he did so by "rediscovering" the Japanese system of printing from multiple woodblocks with water-based pigments. Each of the forty prints from his *Breton Landscapes* series (1889-94) required twenty-five blocks or more; today they represent one of the most intense and accomplished undertakings dedicated to attaining the Japanese spirit in French art.

Mary Cassatt also found inspiration in the color woodblock prints of Japan. She had of course been aware of Japanese prints for many years, and may even have begun collecting them before her visit in April 1890 to the major exhibition of *ukiyo-e* prints at the École des Beaux-Arts.[38] The tremendous impact that this presentation of the history of Japanese prints had on Cassatt is revealed in her letter to Berthe Morisot written that same month: "You could come and dine here with us and afterward we could go to see the Japanese prints at the Beaux-Arts. Seriously, you must not miss that. You who want to make color prints, you could not dream of anything more beautiful. I dream of it and do not think of anything else but color on copper."[39] Cassatt too, one assumes, would have considered the woodblock medium for her purposes. But like Raffaëlli, Maurin, and Pissarro (much more so than the young Rivière), she was well versed in intaglio printmaking techniques prior to her involvement with color printing. It was natural that she sought a means of creating color prints in the medium with which she was most experienced and comfortable, even if it meant adapting these intaglio techniques to processes traditionally reserved for relief printing.

From 1889 to early 1890 Cassatt produced a series of twelve drypoints that she showed along with a group of aquatints in the spring of 1890 in the Peintres-Graveurs exhibition at the Durand-Ruel gallery.[40] In her set of twelve drypoints, Cassatt emphasized the linear qualities

29

The Tub,
1890-91

Mary Cassatt

Bon à 2 épreuves   *Imprimée par l'artiste et Mr Leroy*

Mary Cassatt

36

Mother's Caress,
1890-91
Mary Cassatt

38

The Coiffure,
1891
Mary Cassatt

34

The Toilette,
1890-91
Mary Cassatt

of the technique by limiting the amount of drawing and modeling and allowing the white paper on which each image was printed to be a major part of the composition. The abbreviated lines, suggesting but not fully defining elements in each image such as a wall, chair, table, or figure, and with a Japanese-like reverse perspective, have the simplicity and elegance of the linear effects of Utamaro's eighteenth-century woodblock prints of courtesans.

Cassatt finally realized her dream of printing in color during the second half of 1890, when she embarked upon her series of ten color etchings. They were revealed to the public in April 1891 in the exhibition she organized with Pissarro at the Durand-Ruel gallery in protest of the exclusion of non-French-born artists from the newly reorganized Société des Peintres-Graveurs Français. As Cassatt explained some years later, the set of ten plates was created with the intention of imitating Japanese methods.[41] A simple drypoint composition served as the basic outline of each print before the addition of color plates, and in most cases served as the first state. The final and more complex color composition of nine of the ten images was achieved with two additional plates worked through various stages in softground and aquatint. For the registration and printing of these plates Cassatt requested the expert assistance of the printer Leroy.

Just as the aspatial compositions of Cassatt's color prints related to basic elements of Japanese *ukiyo-e* prints—diagonals, reverse perspectives, overlapping patterns, and a lack of modeling—so too did Cassatt's choice of colors. She favored non-primary colors: oranges, beiges, browns, purples, greens, and when a primary color such as a blue or a yellow was used, it was generally not placed next to another. One exception is Cassatt's first print for the series *The Tub*, in which the blue tub and water are juxtaposed with the mother's yellow dress; but even this color relationship varies within the edition of twenty-five. As the first in the series of ten, *The Tub* was an experiment in imitating Japanese prints, and its direct model is Utamaro's eighteenth-century woodblock version of a mother

32

The Letter,
1890-91
Mary Cassatt

33

The Fitting,
1890-91
Mary Cassatt

31

In the Omnibus,
1890-91
Mary Cassatt

37

Afternoon Tea Party,
1890-91
Mary Cassatt

30

The Lamp,
1890-91
Mary Cassatt

bathing her child in a small basin.[42] Cassatt stated, however, that the nine images that followed had no specific sources; indeed, they are only generically related to the subject, style, composition, and color of *ukiyo-e* prints.[43]

There can be no doubt that Cassatt's ten color etchings were the most significant achievement in the medium to date. Not only did they comprise an original treatment of the theme of bourgeois domesticity, but their modernity was complemented by the assimilation of Japanese compositional elements and color schemes. With the aid of Leroy, Cassatt conquered the problems associated with intaglio color printing, in particular the registration of plates. Her control over the process allowed much greater consistency in the quality of her work which, in turn, undoubtedly inspired in others the confidence to work in the medium. It was hardly a coincidence that in the early 1890s Marie Gautier and Charles Houdard also began to create color etchings with themes and compositions influenced by Japan.

In the spring of 1891, as Cassatt and Pissarro were preparing for their own "salon des refusés" at the Durand-Ruel gallery, Pissarro saw Cassatt's color etchings and reported back enthusiastically to his son Lucien:

"It is absolutely necessary, while what I saw yesterday at Miss Cassatt's is still fresh in mind, to tell you about the colored engravings she is to show at Durand-Ruel's at the same time as I. We open Saturday, the same day as the patriots, who, between the two of us, are going to be furious when they discover right next to their exhibition a show of rare and exquisite works. You remember the effects that you strove for at Éragny? Well, Miss Cassatt has realized just such effects, and admirably: the mat tone, even, subtle, delicate, without stains on seams: adorable blues, fresh rose, etc. We had to have copper plates, a *boîte à grain*, this was a nuisance, but it is absolutely necessary to have uniform and imperceptible grains and a good printer. But the result is admirable, as beautiful as Japanese work, and done with printer's ink!"[44]

Later, on April 25, 1891, Pissarro informed Lucien of another visit to Cassatt's studio,

where she was still printing impressions of the set of ten etchings:

"Her method is the same as ours except that she does not use pure colors, she mixes her tones and thus is able to get along with only two plates. The drawback is that she cannot obtain pure and luminous tones, however her tones are attractive enough. We will have to make a more definitive trial of our own method to determine which is to be preferred."[45]

It is evident from these statements that Pissarro, with the assistance of his son, was seriously if not actively attempting to create color aquatints using the traditional system of combining primary, or "pure," colors. The letter of April 3rd suggests that they had actually attempted to make such prints at Éragny, which would have been prior to Lucien's move to London in November 1890. They were disappointed, however, with the results of their application of aquatint grain because they did not obtain the "mat tone . . . adorable blues, fresh rose . . ."[46] that Pissarro thought Cassatt had achieved so well in her work. Out of Pissarro's total output of five color etchings there is evidence of an aquatint grain only in *The Beggars*. Among his early aquatints, this print alone displays the negative qualities that the artist so hoped to overcome: the crudely applied smudges and patches of aquatint fight against the luminosity and purity of the three primary colors. Indeed, *The Beggars* does not obtain the light and airy impressionist effects of his other color etchings; it is an awkward, experimental print much like the early efforts of Charles Maurin. Although traditionally dated around 1894-95, *The Beggars'* crudeness and use of aquatint rather than pure line etching does not match Pissarro's other color work of that period;[47] based on the brief references to his color etchings in his letters, it seems more accurate to place this print closer to 1890 or 1891, when father and son were first experimenting with color aquatint. By January 1894, however, once Pissarro had purchased an etching press from Delâtre, he was able to produce color etchings to his satisfaction. On January 18, 1895 he relayed the following information to Lucien:

The Beggars,
1890-91
Camille Pissarro

C. P.   no 1/11

50

140a

Little Peasant Girls
in the Grass,
c. 1894
Camille Pissarro

140b

Little Peasant Girls
in the Grass,
c. 1894
Camille Pissarro

n° 4 Ep d'art

marché de Gisors (rue de Cappeville) en 4 planches.

C. Pissarro

141

Market at Gisors
(*rue Cappeville*),
c. 1894

Camille Pissarro

"I received my colored plates, I had had them steeled [steel-faced]. I will send you soon a fine print of my *Little Peasant Girls in the Grass* and a *Market* in black, retouched with tints; I think some excellent things can be made in this way. . . . It bears no resemblance to those of Miss Cassatt, it involves nothing more than retouching with colors, that is all. I have already gotten some fine proofs. . . ."[48]

Therefore, while Cassatt used broad, dominant areas of aquatint grain to create interlocking planes of color that define and finalize the composition, Pissarro, like Raffaëlli, looked to color as a means to highlight an essentially black-and-white line etching, as did their old colleague Bracquemond in his color rendition of his 1893 black-and-white etching *The Rainbow.* Of these two different aesthetic and technical approaches to the medium, the former, introduced by Cassatt and reinforced thereafter by the work of Maurin and Eugène Delâtre, gained a greater number of advocates and underwent a variety of innovative transformations over the subsequent decade as activity in color etching intensified.

The presence of the progressive proofs of Guérard's three-color portrait of his son, Jean Raimond, in the spring 1890 Peintres-Graveurs exhibition, and the publication of the single-color proofs and final image of Guérard's three-color etching *Punchinello* in the September 1890 issue of *Le Livre moderne,* gave Charles Maurin ample opportunity to consider experimenting with printing in red, yellow, blue and black from four plates. His earliest documented color etchings are both dated 1891 in the plate. *The Card*

Player was printed *au repérage* in red, yellow, blue, and black with at least one single impression printed only in blue and black; his 1891 depiction of a young woman combing her hair framed by a Japanese-inspired decorative border is from two plates, this time green and black. In December of that year Maurin, always an avid investigator of printing processes, applied for the patent of the non-intaglio system of printing a multicolor image from one plate under slight pressure from an etching press. This invention did not produce many results, but his simultaneous efforts with printing in color from multiple intaglio plates began to bear fruit.[49] The curious image *Woman and Cat*, although undated, is probably one of his earliest efforts. Like *The Card Player* it was printed from plates produced with varied grains of aquatint combined with etched lines that trace the contours

116

Nude,
1891
Charles Maurin

117

Woman and Cat,
1891
Charles Maurin

of the subject. A trial proof in the collection of the Zimmerli Museum was printed from two plates; the first was inked in black and the second in red. It was also highlighted with blue watercolor overall and with a touch of yellow, barely visible at the back of the woman's waist. Although the red and black colors are in relatively close registration, the horizontal borders of the red plate do not align with those of the black one, suggesting that Maurin was just beginning to learn the system of making multiple plates.

While Maurin was experimenting with printing in the three primary colors and black, so too was his friend Henri de Toulouse-Lautrec. The latter, however, was working in the medium of lithography rather than etching; the first and only time Lautrec used the eighteenth-century three-color scheme to produce a lithographic image

was for his now-famous first poster *Moulin Rouge, La Goulue* of 1891. (He was to use the three-color system again in his photo-relief illustrations for *Le Figaro illustré* and *Le Rire*.) Since this was not the usual color combination for lithographic posters, it seems more than a coincidence that these two artists were simultaneously experimenting with printing in the three primary colors; it is more likely that the older, more knowledgeable, and more active printmaker, Maurin, influenced the young Lautrec to work in this system rather than vice versa.[50]

Another print by Maurin from this period is *Young Girl on a Bench, Sewing*, or *Garden Interior*, printed in red, yellow, blue, and black from four aquatint and softground plates. This undated work is listed in Edmond Sagot's sale catalogue of September 1892 with the indication that only a few proofs were pulled.[51] There is a rough, ex-

79

Mass in Brittany,
c. 1900
Émile-Alfred
Dezaunay

80

Plougastel Daoulas,
c. 1900
Émile-Alfred
Dezaunay

perimental quality to its superimposition of one color plate over the other. Although the plates are registered fairly closely so as to allow the lines, shapes and colors to line up properly, Maurin made several misjudgements. The leaves produced by an aquatint grain on his yellow plate do not connect with any tree or merge with other colors. Similar awkwardnesses occur, as we have seen, in Pissarro's *The Beggars* and also in the trial proof for Eugène Delâtre's *Village of Bevillers*, suggesting that it, too, is an example of early experimentation in creating color intaglio plates. *Village of Bevillers* certainly lacks the technical finesse of works by Delâtre dated as early as 1893. The irregular and unsubtle stopping out of aquatint and of other acid biting is an indication of a lack of control or skill in the application of these tonal etching processes. It seems apparent that this work marks the

97

End of Day,
before 1901
**Charles-Louis
Houdard**

N° 13/15
Ch. Houdard

95

Frogs and Iris,
1894
Charles-Louis
Houdard

entrance of Delâtre into the field of color print-ing, and again it is quite possible that Maurin was the motivation for this important first step by the movement's most influential printer and teacher.

By 1893 printing with the three primary colors —red, yellow, and blue—was no longer prac-ticed by Delâtre or Maurin; this traditional color system had served its instructional purposes for the two, but seemed to thwart rather than en-hance their ability to work in a full spectrum of colors. Besides Pissarro's experiments with col-or etching in 1894-95, few other artists had com-parable success with mixing primary colors from several plates. Charles-Louis Houdard was able to obtain exotic colors for his Japanese-inspired prints, and to create a rich symbolist landscape with the three-color system. Dezaunay and Müller were, however, less successful, and an ornate heaviness prevails in their approaches to

mixing primary pigments from several plates. Most artists, like Mary Cassatt before them, based their work on premixed secondary or ter-tiary colors, sometimes combined with one or more of the three primary colors.

THE INFLUENCE OF EUGÈNE DELÂTRE

At the end of the 1880s Maurin lived in Mont-martre on the rue Gabrielle, just a few blocks from the studio of Auguste Delâtre, who had served for more than forty years as the most highly respected printer of artists' etchings and was an essential participant in the mid-century etching renaissance in France.[52] Auguste's son Eugène worked with him, and from the mid-1880s began to create his own black-and-white etched or drypoint views of Montmartre. Eugène's earliest dated color etching is probably *The Moulins Debray*, printed in red, yellow, blue, plus black and dated 1891 on the plate (a copy of this print is in the Boston Public Library). Maurin, too, etched depictions of his Montmartre surroundings, and both artists continued to do so throughout their careers.

As a member of the small Montmartre community of artistic printmakers, Maurin would have met Eugène when he was making drypoints at the Delâtre studio in the late 1880s. The two, therefore, had been acquainted for some time before they began experimenting together with color etching. The aesthetic incentive probably came initially from the inquisitive Maurin, but the two arrived at technical solutions together. For the rest of the decade, at least, Maurin and Eugène Delâtre maintained a close working relationship. They both contributed to André Marty's 1893 albums of *L'Estampe originale*, and Maurin's aquatint portrait of Toulouse-Lautrec in the first album refers to the former's collaboration with the Delâtre studio in a notation on the plate: "A. Delâtre/Montmartre." Eugène Delâtre was, indeed, a brilliant technician and at times produced work of unusual aesthetic strength, yet he was strongly influenced by those around him, and his art changed from year to year, reflecting the styles and technical innovations of the various artists with whom he worked.

Maurin and Cassatt were the first to influence significantly the subject and style of the younger printer-artist. Delâtre's three-color etching of a child entitled *Portrait of Pauline* is signed "Eug. Delâtre d'après Ch. Maurin 1893," and his color etching *In a Garden* of the same year relates closely to Maurin's earlier version.[53] Delâtre surely visited Cassatt's major retrospective exhibition held at the Durand-Ruel gallery in November and December of 1893. There he would have seen Cassatt's paintings and prints related to her large mural *Modern Woman*, which she had sent earlier that year to the World's Columbian Exposition in Chicago.[54] One such print, a color drypoint and aquatint from three plates entitled *Gathering Fruit*, seems to have made quite an impression on Delâtre. His *Grandfather and Child* is a backyard scene with a vertical and close-to-the-

Richard Ranft
Visiting Card of the Delâtre Household,
Etching
Bibliothèque Nationale

57

In a Garden,
1893
Eugène Delâtre

frontal-plane composition distinctly similar to Cassatt's print. The color schemes (pinks, blues, and greens) also parallel one another. Although the colors in Cassatt's final state of the print are darker than those in Delâtre's work, a preliminary state for *Gathering Fruit*, also included in the exhibition, has lighter colors that are closely related to those of *Grandfather and Child*.[55]

Subjects from Cassatt's 1891 series of color etchings, such as a woman being fitted for a dress or preparing to bathe, are also found in prints by Delâtre and Maurin, but their interpretations of the themes are more sexually alluring. Judging from the much greater emphasis on these seductive images in the *œuvre* of Maurin and his greater predilection for decorated boudoirs colored in dark inks richly applied to the paper by dense areas of aquatint, it was probably he who initiated these pastiches of Cassatt's prints and imparted to Delâtre their overall aesthetics.

There are numerous other examples of Delâtre's exchange with his contemporaries. Delâtre did not just print black-and-white and color; he also provided "information on various etching techniques" and gave "private lessons," as indicated on a business card engraved by Somm depicting a young woman looking at prints by Maurin, Lepère, Leheutre, and Paillard, while the names of Ranft, Geoffroy, Houdard, Rops, Legrand—all clients of Delâtre—are visible below the press.[56] Another business card engraved by Richard Ranft and printed in brown-green ink, depicts a young woman operating a press with, in the background, prints by Houdard, Ranft and Rassenfosse on the walls. A specialty of the Delâtre firm was its "small etching press for artists."[57] We know that Auguste Delâtre sold a press to Mortimer Mempes in 1895 through the intermediary of Armand Séguin[58] and another to Félicien Rops.[59] One year earlier, he sold one to Camille Pissarro,[60] who used it to print his color etchings. Chahine and Robbe also bought presses from Delâtre.[61]

Delâtre's meditative *Portrait of E. Gressin* of 1896 and his *Man Lying in the Grass* refer to the socially oriented images found in the various media of Steinlen; Delâtre's rare depictions of

121

Bathroom,
n.d.
Charles Maurin

123

Intimacy,
n.d.
Charles Maurin

66

*Grandfather
and Child,*
1895
Eugène Delâtre

Singing Lesson,
c. 1901
Eugène Delâtre

cats, colored *à la poupée*, also seemed to occur during his instructional contact with the great cat lover Steinlen, who dedicated *Little Cat* to the printer for introducing him to copper instead of zinc for etchings.

Similarities in subject and in the use of dark green, brown, and black aquatints exist in the work of Delâtre and Manuel Robbe, whose works were printed at the Delâtre studio at the turn of the century. Indeed, as the primary technician for color etching, Delâtre became a transmitter of aesthetic clichés within the large group of artists for whom he served as printer. In a brief discussion that praised printing in col-

or *au repérage* versus *à la poupée*, one critic in 1909 noted the negative results of Delâtre's monopoly on printing:

"Unfortunately most people prefer an easier system [than *au repérage*]. They have a single plate bitten out and deliver it to the printer; on a first proof, printed in bistre, they make a watercolor; then it is the printer's job to determine the series of tones and to apply them on the plate with the dabber, repeating the operation for each printing. Almost all etching *à la poupée* is carried out by a printer of extraordinary skill, Mr. Eugène Delâtre. . . . The prints he produces have a prestigious perfection, but his active involve-

71

*Man Lying in
the Grass,*
c. 1898
Eugène Delâtre

69

*Portrait of
E. Gressin,*
1896
Eugène Delâtre

196

The Sentinel,
1903
Frits Thaulow

163

*Woman on a Chaise
Longue,*
1901
Manuel Robbe

ment also means that they acquire a family resemblance. Mr. Manuel Robbe's Parisian wom-
en, Mr. Francis Jourdain's landscapes, and the
works by more than fifty other artists are of the
same mold, and this monotony compromises
an art so worthy, in all respects, of success."[62]

The more popular or commercial the image
and the larger the edition, the more likely it was
that an expedient artist like Robbe delegated
much of the production of a color etching to
Delâtre. His involvement often went beyond
simply working from an artist's watercolor proof
and printing various colors from one plate *à la
poupée* as described above, to creating additional
color plates with various degrees of participation from the artist. When the skeptical Joseph
Pennell asked Frits Thaulow about his system of
creating color etchings, Thaulow responded:
"Me?—dear sir—all I know is I sign the prints
and I get a check."[63]

Considering the degree of agony Pissarro endured in the process of creating color etchings, it is understandable that large editions, that is, over fifty impressions, were not common for artists who had a personal involvement with the medium, controlling the color and inking their own variations themselves. Cassatt's set of ten color etchings was printed in editions of twenty-five; Villon worked in sizes ranging from ten to twenty-five, thirty, or fifty; Ranft, normally twenty-five; Bottini, twenty-five or forty; Sunyer, thirty; Steinlen, ten to thirty; and Maurin, from five to fifty. The edition sizes of prints by Marie Gautier, Cottet, Krouglicoff, Michl, and Bruyer are seldom known, but were probably quite small, judging from their rarity and their idiosyncratic quality. These quantities contrast with Delâtre's editions of seventy-five or more, Raffaëlli's 100 or more, and the eventual mass production of work, for instance by Gatier, for editions of 250.

185

The House on the Edge of the Village, 1902
Théophile-Alexandre Steinlen

184

Small Cat, 1898
Théophile-Alexandre Steinlen

Edition size, however, is not always a means of judging quality or artistic involvement. Color etchings after all, like other print media, are meant to be multiples, and the artist could still exercise great control over the quality of a large edition, especially if it was printed *au repérage*. This was the case, for instance, with the significant contributions of Delâtre, Lepère, and

Houdard to the albums of L'E*stampe originale,* which had an edition size of at least one hundred.[64] These three prints for the 1893-95 publication possessed a wonderful vibrancy of color because their printer, Delâtre, was not responsible for interpreting color instructions and printing *à la poupée;* even for his own work, *Portrait of Huysmans,* objectivity was important.

Inking and printing multiple intaglio plates, however, were tedious and time-consuming tasks (more than for color lithography, but less than for color woodblock printing); this technical difficulty constrained the medium to relatively limited editions. The demands of the market, however, remained the most decisive factor for the editions of color etchings, and demand did rise toward the turn of the century as dealers responded to the increasing popularity of the medium. In spite of Mary Cassatt's aspira-

tions for her color prints to be affordable to the average person, however, color etching never achieved the high print runs and thus the degree of democratization that color lithography did.[65] Cassatt's labor-intensive, small editions of twenty-five and the production of other color etchers could hardly compete economically with the two or three thousand impressions regularly printed of a poster or, for instance, the thousand impressions of Rivière's large color lithograph, W*inter,* produced for public schools.[66]

Just as lack of control over the printer's interpretation of an artist's pastel or watercolor led to the decline of the color lithographic movement at the end of the 1890s, so by the end of the first decade of the twentieth century, color etching had increasingly fallen prey to loss of artistic originality and to the pressures of large editions.[67] In spite of the efforts of some artists to keep editions low and quality high, such a decline is inevitable when the artist's reliance on craftsmen is greater than his or her curiosity about and contribution to the expressive possibilities of the medium.

In André Mellerio's L*a Lithographie originale en couleurs* of 1898, he describes in detail the participants—artists, printers, dealers—of the then-flourishing color lithography movement.[68] Three

years later Gabriel Mourey published his analysis of "the art of etching in colors," summing up the achievements of those involved.[69] Surprisingly, except for Georges Jeanniot, the artists discussed by Mourey are not among those referred to in Mellerio's article. This is partly due to the fact that neither discourse claims to be encyclopedic, and thus some artists who worked in both media were overlooked because of their relative inactivity in one or the other process at the time of the articles.

While the poster artist Chéret, a member of the Guérard, Pissarro, Raffaëlli, and Cassatt generation, was instrumental in the first stages of the color lithographic movement, its success was assured only when the medium was adopted in the early 1890s by young avant-garde artists such as Pierre Bonnard, Toulouse-Lautrec, Édouard Vuillard and many others, who took advantage of the creative and financial options offered by the medium in the production of posters and theater programs, as well as the opportunity to have their poster art exposed to a massive public in the streets of Paris.

Color etching presented no such financial or audience support systems, and while there were a growing number of sophisticated color lithographic printing facilities available to artists in Paris, in the first half of the decade color etching had only Leroy and Delâtre ready to deal with the complexities of the technique, and even they were learning their way. Initially, therefore, artists involved in color etching persevered for essentially aesthetic reasons. The young avant-garde who finally responded to the medium did so, in general, not during the early part of the decade, when artists such as the Nabis were seeking to combine art and financial remuneration with color lithography, but rather at the end of the decade when publishers and dealers had developed new markets sympathetic to color etching.

In his article "Colored Etchings in France" published in two parts in February and March 1901, Gabriel Mourey concluded: "As one may see, the number of etchers in colors is large; in Paris alone there are from seventy to eighty art-

ists, Frenchmen and foreigners, practicing the art."[70] This is certainly a strong indication that color etching had become an artistic movement of some consequence. The medium was no longer a hidden or mysterious art made complicated by the lack of technical expertise. In 1898, both Raffaëlli and Delâtre had comprehensive shows of their work; even the conservative Salon of the Société des Artistes Français finally, in 1899, accepted prints in color.[71]

COLOR ETCHING IN FIN-DE-SIÈCLE MONTMARTRE

Mourey attributed the revival of color etching to Charles Maurin and specifically *The Card Player* of 1891, Maurin's first attempt in the medium. Curiously, and possibly not by coincidence, its rare subject, a woman playing solitaire, is found again in Villon's *The Cards* of 1903, while its meditative mood of isolation, heightened in the impression printed in blue and black, relates to Picasso's *The Frugal Repast* of 1904. Indeed, the young avant-garde artists

who found refuge in Montmartre at the end of the century relied on Delâtre's facilities and technical expertise, and would easily have encountered Maurin and his etchings at Delâtre's atelier. These artists included Jacques Villon and the young, dissolute Georges-Alfred Bottini, both of whom, like their idol Toulouse-Lautrec, had studied at Cormon's studio on the edge of Montmartre and were involved in the cabaret life of the area. Joining them in their social and aesthetic interests were Joaquin Sunyer, who had arrived in Paris in 1894, and a coterie of other Spaniards—Francisco Iturrino, Ricardo Canals, and finally Picasso—who settled in Paris after enjoying the lively bohemian environment of the El Quatre Gats cabaret in Barcelona.[72]

Théophile-Alexandre Steinlen's realist subject matter, his interest in social issues and mannered style appealed strongly to these young Spaniards. Indeed, he was a major reason for their moving to Montmartre, and they often evoked Montmartre and Steinlen's view of humanity in their early Parisian work.[73] For instance, within a year of the 1897 publication of Jehan Rictus's *Les Soliloques du pauvre* with a cover illustration by Steinlen, Sunyer had created an album of eight color lithographs very much in

206
The Cards,
1903
Jacques Villon

115
The Card Player,
1891
Charles Maurin

188
Secrets,
c. 1990
**Joaquin Sunyer
y Miro**
(Detail on
facing page)

98
Women in the Wood,
c. 1900
Francisco Iturrino

187

The Ragpicker,
1900
**Joaquin Sunyer
y Miro**

186

Shoelace Seller,
1899
**Joaquin Sunyer
y Miro**

the style of Steinlen's own interpretation of the poet's emotional depiction of the harsh realities of poverty.[74] Sunyer would have encountered Rictus and other bohemian poets, composers, and musicians at the Quat'-z-Arts cabaret at 62 boulevard de Clichy where, beginning in December 1893, nightly shows often featured brazen and anti-bourgeois recitals and performances. Rictus himself stunned the clients of the cabaret on the night of December 12, 1896 when he recited for the first time in public the poem "L'Hiver" from his *Les Soliloques du pauvre*, beginning with the now infamous, but no longer quite so provocative line: "Merde! v'la l'hiver et ses dur'tés. . . ."[75]

Sunyer's *The Ragpicker* and *Shoelace Seller* are sympathetic depictions of vagabonds eking out a meager existence by hawking cheap goods from town to town, from one local fair to another, and along the impoverished outskirts of great cities. The prints, each with a hunched foreground figure posed alone against the hovels of the suburbs, found their compositional model and color range in Steinlen's *The Washerwomen*, and ideologically reflect a major theme of Rictus's poem: the sense of isolation and exclusion of the poor from the rest of society. This message is even more poignantly and eloquently implied in Picasso's *The Frugal Repast*, which depicts a couple alone in their own fragile world on the fringe of society. The world of poverty was not

only harsh, but also dangerous, as Steinlen shows in *Prostitute and Pimp*.

The young avant-garde artists and poets in turn-of-the-century Montmartre lived literally and ideologically on the edge of society, and therefore could easily empathize with the destitute and the outcasts of the city, if not always because of their own poverty, at least because of their alienation from established society. In his *Students in the Luxembourg Gardens*, Sunyer stressed the unconventional role of the young artists in typical bohemian black attire with broad-rim hat, mingling with their female friends in a manner more intimate than bourgeois mores allowed. By locating the students at the eastern end of the park with the view of the Pantheon and the Place de la Sorbonne framed in the distance, Sunyer alludes to the radical nature of young artists and students, whose anti-academic and anti-government riots traditionally occurred at this very intersection.[76]

If Sunyer and his colleagues admired Steinlen's anarchist and socialist views of life, they were also fascinated by Toulouse-Lautrec's depictions of the Parisian *demi-monde*: revelers in seedy bars, prostitutes, and other exotic *marginaux*. By living in Montmartre at the Bateau-Lavoir, they became intimate participants in and active contributors to the most radical environment of contemporary art and literature. With the influence of Steinlen's early attempts

Steinlen

181
Prostitute and Pimp,
1898
**Théophile-
Alexandre Steinlen**

189
*Students in the
Luxembourg
Gardens,*
c. 1900
**Joaquin Sunyer
y Miro**

180
The Washerwomen,
1898
**Théophile-
Alexandre Steinlen**

in the medium, color etching was accepted as a legitimate new means of self-expression, a means of creating an art parallel in its extreme nature to the poems of Jehan Rictus or the interpretations of the popular chansonnier Marcel Legay, who performed at the Quat'-z-Arts.[77]

For Bottini in particular, color etching served a sensibility far removed from the gentility of an artist like Mary Cassatt. Bottini used dark tones of brown and black; he left ink smeared on the surface of the plate that printed like a monotype; this was set off by strategically placed dabs of yellow, green or red. When necessary, these spots of color emphasized the vulgarity of an individual or a situation, as in Bottini's depiction of a prostitute dining or putting on makeup at a dinner, or suggested seductiveness, as in his *Reclining Woman*, or exotic eroticism, as in Villon's *Negro Made Good*.

The work of Bottini, Sunyer, Iturrino, Jourdain, Villon, Müller, Chahine, Krouglicoff, Robbe, and, by 1906, the seascapes of Cottet were created with a very personal manipulation of surface inks and with dark or subdued colors printed from irregularly bitten and scraped plates. Concurrently, however, the inheritance of Cassatt's

9
Boxing Match,
n.d.
Georges-Alfred Bottini

45
The Tightrope Walker,
1906
Edgar Chahine

191
Marcel Legay,
c. 1900
Joaquin Sunyer y Miro

10

Supper,
n.d.
**Georges-Alfred
Bottini**

7

La Soupeuse,
1903
**Georges-Alfred
Bottini**

198

Negro Made Good,
1899

Jacques Villon

4

Reclining Woman,
1898

**Georges-Alfred
Bottini**

The Cakewalk,
1903
**Georges-Alfred
Bottini**

George Botter 1900

129
At *the Moulin-Rouge*,
c. 1900
Alfredo Müller

14
*Brittany Peasant
Woman*,
1900
**Bernard Boutet
de Monvel**

broad aquatint planes of color could be found in the work of Boutet de Monvel, Villon, and Taquoy. Thus, while the patterns of color aquatint reach an almost Mondrian-like abstraction in Boutet de Monvel's *Brittany Peasant Woman*, Villon's *The Cards* combines the color schemes, patterns, and compositional elements of Cassatt's domestic, bourgeois interior scenes with the decadent subject matter associated with Toulouse-Lautrec and Bottini. While Cassatt depicted a middle-class woman sitting at a desk dutifully writing a letter, Villon portrayed a prostitute biding her time playing solitaire, and

while the image of an adored child played a role in four of the American artist's 1890-91 series, the companion for Villon's woman is a pet dog. From housewife to whore, from Brittany peasant to aristocratic huntsman, from urban proletarian to cabaret performer, from views of Paris to sea- and landscapes, distinct interpretations of *fin-de-siècle* subject matter are found in the medium of color etching. Even humorous caricature, normally the domain of lithography or photomechanical journal illustration in France, was practiced to a limited extent in the intaglio medium by Boutet and colored *à la poupée*.

13

Plaisir d'amour. . . ,
c. 1895
Henri Boutet

12

Oui, Monsieur le Comte. . . ,
c. 1895
Henri Boutet

24

Chaff,
1906
Georges Bruyer

194

Two Hounds,
1906
Maurice Taquoy

195

Two Pointers,
1907
Maurice Taquoy

156

Morning Walk,
c. 1900
Richard Ranft

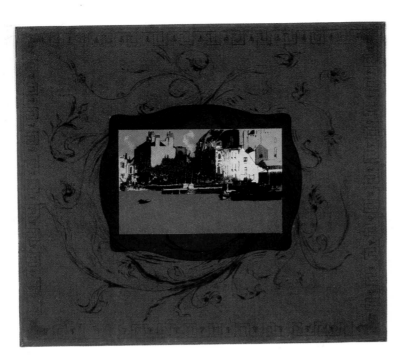

The Chelsea Palaces,
c. 1890-97
Théodore Roussel
(Detail on
facing page)

NEW TENDENCIES AT THE TURN
OF THE CENTURY

In 1900 Théodore Roussel published a portfolio of nine color etchings produced during the preceding decade. Unlike the series of ten color etchings by Cassatt and the lithograph albums of the 1890s by artists such as Toulouse-Lautrec, Redon, Bonnard, Vuillard, and others, each a group of prints with an underlying theme, Roussel's portfolio of miniature color aquatint images serves as a summation of a number of thematic concerns in France and England at the end of the century: landscape, seascape, still life, the nude, Oriental motifs.[78] Besides the medium, the common denominator of Roussel's prints is their unusual presentation: an impression of each small image is hinged with glue onto a much larger sheet of paper, etched in color with a decorative motif or cartouche that seems to frame the image. Roussel created a Lilliputian museum filled with such colorful gems as a Redon-like still life, a Sisley-like landscape, a Vuillard-like view through a window, and a Whistleresque view of Chelsea. The eclectic subject matter of the portfolio is, however, endowed with a truly personal approach to the medium, and has resulted in a highly original response to a wide range of turn-of-the-century aesthetic concerns.

At its best, color etching was an intimate medium that lent itself to many creative possibilities. Some artists, such as Cassatt, Maurin, Houdard, Roussel, and Villon, stretched it to new technical limits, while others such as Buhot, Signac, Bottini, Cottet, and Picasso exploited its minimal means of expressiveness and suggestion. In 1879, when Pissarro and Degas experimented with printing several impressions of *Dusk with Haystacks* in single colors, they were seeking to suggest simply the visual changes in nature caused by the effects of light at different times of day. They thus created a sequence of distinctly different landscape views without altering the basic matrix of the aquatint, etching, and drypoint plate. As such, these single color etchings are extraordinary accomplishments in the history of Impressionism, and are important precursors of Monet's 1891 sequence of haystacks and of the Rouen Cathedral paintings some years later.[79]

Signac's *Flessingue*, a wonderfully subtle seascape defined by a multitude of threadlike, quivering etched lines, was printed in blue in an edition of fifteen; in one impression, however, Signac experimented with producing the effects of a fine vertical rain by superimposing a second plate slightly abraded and inked with a gray tint. Going one step, or rather, one color further than had Degas and Pissarro, Signac was pleased with the effect he had achieved and signed and numbered the print "no. 12" of the edition. One of the attractive qualities of color etching for artists like Signac was the ability to achieve different effects in the same composition by either adding or alternating the colors, *à la poupée*, or by adding plates or changing a plate's color. Ranft's *Return from the Costume Ball*, Delâtre's *Woman with a Parasol*, and Steinlen's *Reclining Nude* are examples in which artists included, within the regular edition of the print, variations on the coloration of the image, not intending these changes to be mere trial proofs. On the other hand, the trial proofs of Villon and Cottet for *On a Bench* and *Boats*, with their subtle differences in color from the editioned print, indicate just how important it was for these artists to achieve the right color effect.

On the other hand, while lithographic artists

183b

Reclining Nude,
1898
**Théophile-
Alexandre
Steinlen**

183a

Reclining Nude,
1898
**Théophile-
Alexandre
Steinlen**

202a

On a Bench,
1900
Jacques Villon

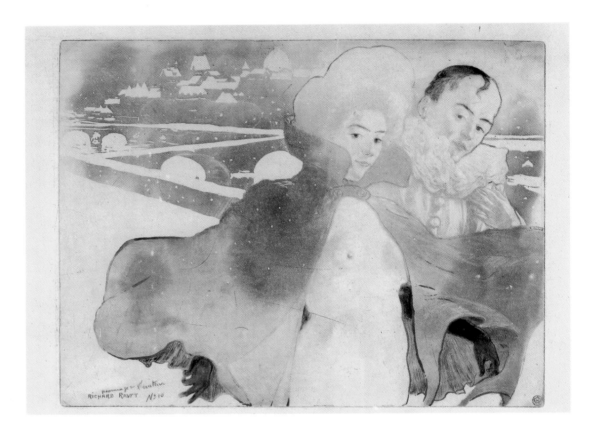

155a

Return from the
Costume Ball,
c. 1900
Richard Ranft

155b

Return from the
Costume Ball,
c. 1900
Richard Ranft

found strong and often arbitrary color an effective means of creating the visual impact necessary for an attention-getting poster or program, color etchers also made forceful images as they ventured away from the traditional descriptive function of color. They experimented with ways to emphasize the intensity of color: the symbolic or arbitrary relationship of color to subject, the isolation of colors against the white of the paper, or the interjection of a patch of vivid color within a more neutral overall tonality. From Guérard's masks and Delâtre's symbol of syphilitic death to Lepape's new-age automobile, these bold visual statements, though on a smaller physical scale, were in keeping and competitive with many of the aesthetic concerns of their contemporary sister arts—postermaking and painting.

In contrast to color lithography, the medium of color etching rarely took on the purely decorative qualities now associated with the term Art Nouveau—an emphasis on flat pattern, curvilinear line, pastel colors, and floral motifs. Instead, a consistent feature of the medium was the texture produced by aquatint, softground, and various other acid bite techniques. In Gautier's *Saint-Briac*, rough, abstract, liquid aquatint and softground textures play across the surface of the print and serve to evoke the sea and clouds, suggesting that Gautier's true interest was tactile rather than representational. Delâtre's cover for Maufra's *Brittany* album mixes line etching with liquid, irregularly applied, broad-grain aquatint to render Japanese-inspired spewing waves and a textured surface that is further heightened by flat, poster-like letters.

111

At the Seaside,
1906
Georges Lepape

84

Saint-Briac,
c. 1893
Marie Gautier

61

In Brittany, Etchings and Lithographs by Maufra,
1894
Eugène Delâtre

70

Death Wearing Furs,
c. 1897
Eugène Delâtre

114

Château de Lavardin,
1908
Maxime Maufra

As one finds in the earlier black-and-white prints of Goya, Degas, Pissarro, and Cassatt, the textures and grains obtained by the application of aquatint, softground, pure acid and so forth, cause the viewer to concentrate on the textured surface of the print, sometimes at the expense of the image itself. Müller's dynamic portrait of Suzanne Despres in his *Two Girls Playing in a Garden*, and Joseph Pinchon's *Dog* focus attention on the foreground surface through the texture of the intaglio medium and the simplified broad planes and shapes of color defined by these textures of acid bite.

A comparison of two prints immediately reveals how the physical properties of tonal intaglio processes functioned to create works of greater abstraction and, thus, a greater degree of modernity. Lepère's light and airy *Landing Stage on the Garonne, Bordeaux* of 1897 is essentially a line etching with descriptive color depicting in a representational linear style an elegant young woman descending the ramp of a passenger boat. Although the frontal plane of the composition is emphasized by the bold figure of the woman, Lepère has created a traditional landscape. In contrast, Bruyer's *The Duenna* was produced almost entirely in textures of aquatint that simplify

and flatten the figures, limit the space, and create planes of silhouettes as in a shadow theater, all of which was quite modern in approach.

Betout's *The Wrestlers*, though darker and more tonal, was traditionally rendered, much in the same descriptive, linear manner as Lepère's *Landing Stage on the Garonne, Bordeaux*. However, if Betout had stopped his work on this print at its third state, with aquatint grain dominating line etching, his final concept would have been much closer to Bruyer's silhouetted composition and to the planar and more abstract qualities exhibited so dramatically in Steinlen's *Parasol*, in Francis Jourdain's *Woman in the Shade* and in Müller's *Two Girls Playing in a Garden*. The avoidance of strict topographical or realistic depiction is one sign of artistic modernity at the turn of the century; ironically, the combination of color and tonal intaglio processes, for so long analogous with reproductive printmaking, offered a unique means to achieve this avant-garde end. It is clear, however, that color etching's traditional and modern attributes coexisted. Helleu's delicate line-etched portrait of a fashionable woman has all the qualities of a finely drawn and modeled academic study, while Robbe's color aquatint depiction of a connoisseur of prints attains the chiaroscuro bravura of a painting. In contrast, Michl's simple, unmodeled line sketch accentuated with black and purple aquatint, and Villon's *On a Bench* and *Mlle. Ellen Andrée*, both primarily in aquatint, emphasize the innate physical character of the intaglio medium rather than its ability to achieve verisimilitude.

As we have seen, the period 1890 to 1910 marks the first foray of a large number of artists into the technical and aesthetic investigation of color etching. Although overshadowed at the time by the more prolific and monumental activities in color lithography, this veritable movement resulted in a significant body of creative work. The color etching movement provides strong evidence of the intense quest by turn-of-the-century artists for an innovative, personal means to express rapidly changing and diverse artistic attitudes. Its achievement meant that the medium was freed forever from its designation as a purely reproductive technique.

136

Dog,
c. 1900
Joseph-Porphyre Pinchon

Suzanne Despres
in Poil de Carotte,
c. 1900
Alfredo Müller

113

Landing Stage on the
Garonne, Bordeaux,
1897
Auguste Lepère

26

The Duenna,
c. 1906
Georges Bruyer

3a

The Wrestlers,
1899
Clément Bétout

3b

The Wrestlers,
1899
Clément Bétout

Jacques Villon
2/30

94

*Portrait of
Madeleine Carlier,*
c. 1904
Paul Helleu

200

Mlle. Ellen Andrée,
1900
Jacques Villon

182

Parasol,
1898
**Théophile-
Alexandre Steinlen**

125

The Trinket,
1907
Victor Mignot

124

At the Café,
1900
Ferdinand Michl

ED. SAGOT

THE EXPANSION
OF COLOR ETCHING IN PARIS

1895-1914: THE ROLE OF PUBLISHERS AND DEALERS

Some dealers played an essential role in the creation and promotion of color etching. The first was, of course, Paul Durand-Ruel; he was the recognized dealer for the Impressionists, for Pissarro and for Mary Cassatt. Cassatt left her prints with him on consignment and referred clients to him. In fact, the exhibitions organized by the Société des Peintres-Graveurs were held in Durand-Ruel's gallery. He was one of the rare dealers who was accepted by Pissarro, an artist who was not generally well-disposed toward members of this profession: "The French dealers are astonishing. I went to see Sagot, a dealer in prints. He asked me for etchings and made an incredible remark: 'I used to like your *Série des pouilleux*, but you were asking too much for them.' 'Oh!' I replied, 'but I'm asking twice as much for them now.' They were thirty francs then! What do you think of that? . . . We ruin ourselves so that these dealers can make a fortune. . . . And God knows they do. Sagot is remarkably well established in the rue de Chateaudun; he sells the Grasset posters and other monstrosities to collectors. It's the fashion!" (letter of March 14, 1895).[1]

On the subject of Ambroise Vollard, Pissarro wrote to his son Lucien on July 3, 1896: "This amazing Vollard has incredible ambitions. He wants to start selling prints and all the dealers, Sagot, Dumont, etc., are fighting him intensely because he wants to upset their little business . . . but I'm afraid he's going to get his fingers burnt! . . . In any case, we mustn't fool ourselves."[2] Pissarro's suspicions were, in fact, well

founded, as he wrote on July 18, 1896: "No, really, they take us for idiots! Work hard, my boy, work, search, and we will take care of making the money!" In the same letter to Lucien he wrote that "there is nothing to be done, no more with Vollard than with Bing, Sagot, and *tutti quanti*, unless we allow ourselves to be fleeced."[3]

Instead, Pissarro left etchings on consignment with Gutbier, director of the Arnold company in Dresden; when Gutbier managed to sell two black-and-white etchings, Pissarro gloated to Lucien: "I sold *The Hovel* for 100 francs and

193

Ed. Sagot,
1906
Maurice Taquoy

Manuel Robbe
Invitation for
an exhibition
of prints at
Edmond Sagot's,
1903
Etching
and aquatint
Bibliothèque
Nationale

Bathing Goosegirls,
c. 1895
Camille Pissarro

the other [*The Stone Bridge*] for 75 francs. Vollard, who felt that 150 for a color etching was too expensive, was astounded!" (letter of September 2, 1896). But Gutbier told Pissarro: "I've had bad experiences with series—all my collectors like to purchase a few sheets, that's what they like and no more; the same goes for our institutions. I would be very grateful if you would allow me to sell them separately."[4] Vollard had also made this request and, at the time, Pissarro refused.

Beginning on March 15, 1897, *L'Estampe et l'Affiche* began to follow the market for color etchings in its column "Les Estampes et les affiches du mois." The dealers regularly cited by the critic Georges Riat were Ambroise Vollard (6 rue Laffitte), Gustave Pellet (9 quai Voltaire), Edmond Sagot (39 bis rue de Chateaudun), Charles Hessèle (13 rue Laffitte), and Kleinmann (8 rue de la Victoire). Herein we learn

that Vollard published *Dancer at the Bar* by Gustave Leheutre, an edition of twenty-five selling at 25 francs each. He also published the *Album des peintres-graveurs*, which included two color etchings by Leheutre and Maurin; printed in an edition of 100, it sold for 150 francs. In December 1897-January 1898, he published the *Album d'estampes originales de la galerie Vollard*, an edition of 100 prints that sold for 400 francs, including only one color etching: *Eve*, by Maurin.

In February 1897, Gustave Pellet published *Little Class* and *Sentimental Education* by Maurin, two series of eight color drypoints on japan paper. He also sold engraved color reproductions for surprisingly high prices. Albert Bertrand printed three color etchings, after Félicien Rops, in February 1897. Each print of *Pornocrates or Woman with Pig*, a single edition of 115 impressions (the plates were effaced) sold for 300 francs; *Eritis similes Deo, Eve and the Serpent* and *Impudence*, editions of thirty annotated and numbered prints, sold for 150 francs, while 100 prints without annotations sold for 100 francs.

In January and February of 1899, Pellet exhibited Bertrand's print *Embarkation for Cythera*, after Watteau. The publicity was well planned. L'*Estampe et l'Affiche* published an article about the exhibition: "A color etching by Bertrand is now showing at the Pellet gallery, 9 quai Voltaire, after E*mbarkation for Cythera* by Watteau. The talented interpreter of *Scandal* has accomplished this new and difficult task admirably, using no less than four plates and registering them precisely, to achieve the remarkable effects that we can see today. M. Bertrand spent two years working to achieve this result. By the way, we would like to mention the attractive invitation, which features a color reproduction of *La Finesse* from the La Caze collection by the same artist. It is a delicate little print, for which collectors should thank Mr. Pellet. . . ." It was not surprising that, as a result of this avalanche of compliments, the fifty de luxe impressions on japan with *remarques*, each priced at 200 francs, were soon sold out. The remaining seventy-five impressions on japan without *remarques* sold for 175 francs each, and the prints on ordinary paper for 120 francs, although the size of this edition was not mentioned.

Meanwhile Edmond Sagot published Bracquemond's *The Rainbow*. Here again, we can evaluate the difference between a print pulled on rare paper and one on ordinary paper (three times less expensive), or between a black-and-white print and a color print. The edition of twenty-five etchings was numbered and signed, and the plate was canceled. Prints on parchment (numbered one to ten) sold for 150 francs, while prints on Japanese vellum, Holland paper, or older paper (numbered eleven to twenty-five) sold for 100 francs. Some of the states sold for 50 francs each. L'*Estampe et l'Affiche* of March 1897 announced: "There were experiments with multiplate color printings and new combinations of techniques; all these impressions are different from one another, and therefore unique. The price varies from 50 to 200 francs, depending on the print. Finally, a

unique collection consisting of the original black-and-white drawing, the etching (impression from the fifth state), a color proof, and six proofs of different colors is priced at 375 francs."

In 1897 Charles Hessèle went into business at 13 rue Laffitte. "A new print and book dealer warmly recommended by Cousturier . . . and a former employee of Firmin-Didot, very well-versed in the field," was Pissarro's judgement of November 26, 1897. In March-April 1898 he published *Girl with Doll* by Maurin, an edition of twenty-seven on Japanese vellum, which sold for 25 francs. In September of the same year, he published *Women Peeling Vegetables* by Ranft (edition of twenty-five, 15 francs), and in November-December, *The Black Cockerel* (edition of twenty, 20 francs), *Swiss Landscape* (edition of ten, 10 francs) and *Nocturne* (edition of twenty, 15 francs) by Jourdain. In December 1898-January 1899, he published *Polo* by Jeanniot (edition of five on Holland paper, 50 francs) and *Young Man* by Boutet de Monvel. Finally, in October 1899 he published Potter (eleven color etchings, 25 to 35 francs), Ey'Chenne, and Van Muyden.

Steinlen's works were sold by Kleinmann: E*rrand Girl in the Rain* (edition of thirty, 25 francs),

Louis Legrand
Invitation for
*Exposition des
dernières œuvres
de Louis Legrand* at
Gustave Pellet's,
1906
Etching
and aquatint
Bibliothèque
Nationale

Charles Maurin
Invitation for
Henri Detouche's
exhibition at
Charles Hessèle's,
n.d.
Aquatint and
softground
Bibliothèque
Nationale

Albert Bertrand
after Watteau
La Finette,
Invitation for
*Exposition de la
gravure en couleurs
de Bertrand
"L'Embarquement
pour Cythère"
de Watteau,*
1898
Etching and
softground
Bibliothèque
Nationale

Francis Jourdain,
Charles Hessèle's
visiting card,
n.d.
Etching and
softground
Bibliothèque
Nationale

The Washerwomen (25 francs), *Prostitute in the Rain* (20 francs). In September-October, 1898, he sold more prints by Steinlen: *Nude on a Sofa* (edition of twenty-five, canceled plates, 30 francs) and *Marton et Pierreuse* (edition of twenty-five, canceled plates, 25 francs). Etchings colored *à la poupée* were proportionally more expensive, such as *Fishing Boat* by Müller (edition of forty, 20 francs) and *Model's Rest* by Robbe.

Finally, in 1888, Georges Petit took over a company founded by Francis Petit in 1846 at 8 rue de Sèze and 12 rue Godot-de-Mauroy

(where he installed his printing shop). He sold works by Houdard, Jourdain, Müller, Pinchon, Robbe, Thaulow, Delâtre, Helleu, Raffaëlli, Jeanniot, and Gatier. Each year he published a catalogue with fixed prices which, generally, remained stable from 1906 to 1911. However, the prices for well-known artists such as Raffaëlli and Robbe rose slowly but steadily. *The Snow, The Storm,* and *The Little Donkeys* by Raffaëlli, in editions of 200, were worth 100 francs in 1907, and 125 in 1911. *Parisian, Color Print,* and *In the Studio* by Robbe, editions of 200, were worth 50 francs in 1907, and 60 in 1911. Some of the editions sold out: *Hélène* and *Gracieuse,* by Helleu, editions of 100, were sold for 100 francs each in 1907 and were all sold by 1911. The public was particularly fond of Chabanian, Helleu, Houdard, Jourdain, Latenay, Le Gout-Gérard, Luigini, Simon, and Thaulow, many of whose plates were unavailable. But success led some particularly greedy artists to enlarge their editions. Pinchon, who in 1914 announced an edition of thirty for *At the Kennels, On the Move, Back at the Château, Breaking Cover,* and *Death of the Stag,* had by 1911 increased the edition to 150 for the first, with the significant annotation "unlimited edition" for the rest, although they all sold for the same price, 20 to 30 francs!

Georges Petit often sold works for less money than did the artist himself during a Salon. In 1906, Pellet was offering *Fishing Boat at Night* by Cottet for 50 francs, whereas it had been sold for 80 francs at the Salon of the Société de la

58b

Bust of Parisian Woman,
1893
Eugène Delâtre

56

On the Boulevards,
1893
Eugène Delâtre

68

At the Café-Concert,
c. 1895
Eugène Delâtre

132
Fishing Fleet,
1902
Alfredo Müller

128
Portrait of Woman
with Straw Hat,
c. 1900
Alfredo Müller

93
Hydrangeas,
c. 1896
Paul Helleu

Henri Guérard
Invitation for
Henri Guérard's
exhibition at
La Bodinière,
1896
Etching and
aquatint
Bibliothèque
Nationale

Gravure Originale en Couleurs one year before. The same phenomenon occurred with *Sunset on Port-de-Bouc* by Picabia (80 and 100 francs) and *Rue de la Paix* by Gatier (60 and 100 francs). The difference was due to the commission paid by the artist to his dealer. As Pissarro explained to the German dealer Gutbier in 1896:

"You currently have ten prints on consignment. My list does not match the prices you have indicated to me for the four prints you would like to purchase. They are marked at 100 francs, the public price, and not 75 francs, but having accepted a price of 50 francs for you I will not retract; I will, however, make my own conditions in the future. If I lower my prices to the public, I will be forced to do the same in England and elsewhere I have sold for the prices on my list."[5]

The dealers also played an important role in organizing exhibitions to promote the work of their artists. The first such dealer was Bernheim (8 rue Laffitte) who in 1887 exhibited twenty-three color etchings by Guérard, including *Twenty Grotesque Masks*, *In the Garden*, and *Punchinello*.

In April of 1891, Durand-Ruel (16 rue Laffitte) exhibited a series of ten prints (drypoint and aquatint) by Mary Cassatt: *The Bath*, *The Lamp*, *In the Omnibus*, *The Letter*, *The Fitting*, *The Toilette*, *Mother's Kiss*, *Maternal Caress*, *Afternoon Tea Party*,

49

*Boats in the Harbour
at Sunset,*
1905
Charles Cottet

Bodinière and Boussod-Valadon. La Bodinière (18 rue Saint-Lazare) exhibited Ranft on January 5, 1892 and Guérard from May 11 to 30, 1896. Boussod-Valadon exhibited works by Maurin from January 30 to February 11, 1893. Vollard showed these same works from September 15 to October 31, 1895, and also devoted an exhibition to Müller.

Born in Hamburg in 1838, Siegfried Bing was involved in an important porcelain and glass concern in Hamburg and Paris. He developed a passionate interest for the decorative arts, and especially Asian art; by the 1870s he had formed a sizable collection and established an international reputation as a scholar and connoisseur of Far Eastern art. In 1894 he voyaged to the United States to study American industrial and decorative arts under the auspices of the Union Centrale des Arts Décoratifs, and his contacts with the interior decorating firm of Louis Comfort Tiffany inspired him to open his own gallery of painting and modern decorative arts in Paris in December 1895. Pissarro wrote to Lucien on May 26,

35

Mother's Kiss,
1890-91
Mary Cassatt

104

The Sea,
c. 1900
Francis Jourdain

and *Study.* He gave her another show in November-December 1893, in which he showed *The Kitchen Garden* and *The Banjo Lesson* in addition to the ten prints previously exhibited. In 1898, Durand-Ruel exhibited etchings by Eugène Delâtre and Francis Jourdain. L'*Estampe et l'Affiche* reviewed the show, criticizing Delâtre because "we cannot condone this work that combines pure etching, existing on its own merit, with hand-coloring added later," but praising Jourdain's work, in which "the inexperience is evident, but the conviction much greater." Among the other precursors were La

131

Montmartre,
rue Saint-Vincent
in Winter,
c. 1900
Alfredo Müller

Alfredo Müller
Invitation for
Alfredo Müller's
exhibition
at Ambroise
Vollard's,
n.d.
Etching and
aquatint
Bibliothèque
Nationale

110b

The Idiot and
the Dancer,
c. 1895
Louis Legrand

including work by Bracquemond, Raffaëlli, and Leheutre.

One of the great turn-of-the-century exhibitions was held at Devambez's gallery (43 boulevard Malesherbes) from November 25 to December 15, 1907. It featured the new color etchings by Raffaëlli, including *Breakfast*, *Gentleman Having Just Painted His Gate*, *The Knife Grinder*, and three works for which the entire edition

1895: "Bing is establishing a business for paintings; he has a gallery now where he once had his Japanese collection. It looks as though he will have a clerk, someone like Van Gogh, as [Bing] is a friend of Théo. This movement is oriented toward the younger artists: Lautrec, Théo [Van Rysselberghe], Signac. . . ."[6] In April 1896, Bing exhibited paintings, drawings, drypoints, and etchings by Legrand in his Art Nouveau gallery. Edmond de Goncourt saw this show and wrote (April 16):

"The interest of this exhibition lies in the figures of the engraved dancers or, even better, the child dancers, in which you can see the vulgarity of the limbs . . . the coarse anatomies, the working-class faces, the alcoholic ancestry behind the shapes and curves of these young girls who pursue an art of grace—and all this is revealed through the powerful magic of a theatrical chiaroscuro drawing; unfortunately, the grain sometimes makes these prints look somewhat like industrial engravings."[7]

The year 1898 was a year of great controversy over color versus black-and-white etching, even though dealers were working hard to promote color etchings. A. Arnould (7 rue Racine) exhibited drypoints by Boutet; Bing, twenty-four etchings by Raffaëlli; Hessèle, drawings, etchings, and pastels by Jeanniot; Pellet, engravings by Bertrand after Watteau; and Sagot, etchings by Maurin and an exhibition of modern prints,

146

Breakfast,
1895
**Jean-François
Raffaëlli**

144

Self-Portrait,
1893
**Jean-François
Raffaëlli**

No. 1019 r Raffaëlli

sold out, *Self-Portrait* (edition of 110, printed in 1893), *To Your Health, Mother Good Times!*, and *The Actress* (edition of sixty, from five plates, printed in 1898).

THE ROLE OF ETCHING SOCIETIES

From 1889, the role of etching societies assumed greater importance. In 1889, the Société des Peintres-Graveurs was founded, with Félix Bracquemond as president, and the first exhibitions were held in the Durand-Ruel gallery. Artists participating in these shows included, among others, Camille Pissarro and Mary Cassatt. In 1891, under the influence of Bracquemond and Guérard, it became the Société des Peintres-Graveurs Français, but still invited several foreign artists to each of its exhibitions. This provoked a dispute between Pissarro and Cassatt; nonetheless she exhibited at the La Bodinière and Devambez galleries and, indeed, received the ultimate honor of an exhibition at the Grand Palais in 1905. A catalogue was printed for all the exhibitions; these documents are now useful in tracing the role of this

The Knife Grinder,
1907
**Jean-François
Raffaëlli**

The Quay of the
Hôtel de Ville,
1899
Eugène Béjot

To Your Health:
Mother Good Times!,
1905
**Jean-François
Raffaëlli**

Between Paris
and Charenton,
1899
Eugène Béjot

130

pioneering society. Color etching was established in its own right from the beginning of the society, due primarily to the influence of Henri Guérard, vice-president from 1890.

The Société des Amis de l'Eau-Forte, founded in January 1897, was essentially an association of collectors. Housed at 10 rue de la Terrasse in Paris, its goal was to purchase previously unpublished plates. Every year, it printed several editions of approximately one hundred impressions, which were then distributed to each member. In 1899, *Dawn* by Charles Coppier was printed; in 1908, *Meeting of Actors in a Park* by Bertrand, after Pater; and in 1912, *Errand Girl* (*Boulevard de la Madeleine*, 1911) by Malo-Renault.

The most important of these societies was the Société de la Gravure Originale en Couleurs, presided by Jean-François Raffaëlli. In 1913, he described the beginnings of the Salon:

"I was feeling discouraged when in 1900 I left for a long trip to America and told my young friends, 'I'm sorry, but all the doors are closed, I can't find any gallery that will put on our exhibition.' But then color etchings began to appear here and there in various exhibitions and the public was interested, and even began to buy. Several years had passed when, one day, I met Georges Petit, who asked me, 'Didn't you come to see me three or four years ago offering to organize an annual exhibition of color etchings?' 'Yes!' 'Well, what if I gave you my big room for one month every year for a show of color etchings? What would you say?' 'I'd say that I accept wholeheartedly and eagerly!' And the color etching Salon was founded!"[8]

From 1904 to 1920, eleven Salons were held, all in George Petit's gallery. In the preface to the first catalogue, Georges Lecomte wrote,

41/65   Manuel-Robbe

109
*Return from
the Shoot,*
c. 1892
Louis Legrand

107
*Woman with
Umbrella,*
c. 1887
Louis Legrand

"Fifty etchers have devoted themselves totally to this Salon. Despite the goal that unites them, it is easy to perceive their diversity of temperament and technique. They almost all differ in method as well as vision and sensibility. The one element they have in common is a desire to revive color etching and to interpret, through its resources, the people and subjects of their times."

In 1908 the society included such dissimilar artists as Adhémar, Béjot, Bellanger, Besnard, Borrel, Bracquemond, Delâtre, Delcourt, Detouche, East, Marie Gautier, Godin, Houdard, Huard, Jeanniot, Jourdain, La Touche, Legrand, Lhermitte, Mac Laughlan, Müller, Piet, Pinet, Prouvé, Raffaëlli, Rivière, Robbe, and Thaulow. Members ranged from some of the most dedicated creators to the most commercial engravers.

The size of the editions also varied considerably, from ten impressions for *Mouse and Carnations* by Marie Gautier, to 250 impressions for *Snow in Normandy* by Bertrand after a work by Thaulow. Furthermore, the price varied according to the rarity: *Effects of the Moon (Étretat)* by Delâtre, an edition of 200, sold for 80 francs, while *Landscape at Saint-Ouen*, also by Delâtre

but a single edition, sold for 125 francs. *Remarques* and "symphonic margins" increased the price: *Avenue of Tall Trees (Saint Cloud)* and *Fountain* by Müller, editions of 124, were worth 80 francs. But it was noted that "for each of these last two plates there will be an edition of twenty-five impressions that will be annotated with a *remarque* consisting of an original drawing by the artist." In this case, a print was worth 100 francs. The wide range of prints and the catalogue that accompanied each exhibition were designed to attract both amateurs and collectors.

The first Salon was held November 6-30, 1904. It consisted of 277 works, including *The Quay of the Hôtel de Ville* by Béjot (edition of twenty-five, 30 francs each); *Old Man Sitting* (edition of thirty, 30 francs) and *The Bar* (edition of thirty, 35 francs) by Boutet de Monvel; *To the Glory of the Cat* by Detouche (edition of forty, 100 francs); *Gentleman Having Just Painted His Gate* by Raffaëlli (edition of 150, 100 francs); *Claudine* by Robbe (edition of sixty-five, 25 francs); *Anemones, China,* and *Summer* by Roussel (edition of seventy-five, expensively priced at 225, 575 and 475 francs); and seventeen etchings by Villon, including *Society Comedy, Cards, Cakewalk* and

A LA GLOIRE DU CHAT

174

Anemones,
1897
Théodore Roussel

173

China,
1896-97

Théodore Roussel

83

Mouse,
c. 1893

Marie Gautier

138

201
Sulking,
1900
Jacques Villon

208
Cakewalk,
1904
Jacques Villon

205
Society Comedy,
1903
Jacques Villon

Comédie de Société   Jacques Villon

48

*Fishermen Fleeing
the Storm,*
c. 1905
Charles Cottet

151

*Factories in
the Snow,*
1909

**Jean-François
Raffaëlli**

Sulking (editions of twenty-five to fifty impressions, 20 to 60 francs).

The second Salon, held November 1-15, 1905, included 211 works: eleven etchings by Charles Cottet; *Mouse* by Marie Gautier (edition of ten, 50 francs); nine etchings by Müller; *To Your Health, Mother Good Times!* by Raffaëlli (edition of 100, 100 francs or 130 francs with frame); and four etchings by Villon (this was the last time he exhibited).

The 1906 Salon included works by Delâtre, Detouche, Marie Gautier, Raffaëlli, Robbe, Roux-Champion, Taquoy, Thaulow, and Francis Picabia, who showed his work again in 1907 with Raffaëlli (*The Knife Grinder*, edition of fifty, 100 francs), Ranft, and Robbe. In 1908, Roger-Milès wrote in his preface to the Salon catalogue that "each year the number of visitors to the Salon of the Société de l'Estampe Originale en Couleurs increases. Everyone has his favorite artist, a fortunate situation because the editions are strictly limited and the impressions with a *remarque*, or those that feature an original watercolor, different for each print, a most interesting technical innovation, are rarer still. From now on, color etching will no longer be an intruder. It has proven itself, it commands at-

tention, it rules, it has conquered its last opponents. . . ."

Among these visitors was the great couturier Jacques Doucet, who regularly purchased prints at each Salon: he spent 340 francs in 1905 and 1,105 francs in 1905. His tastes ran to the traditional, and among his favorites were La Touche, Bompard, Chabanian, Eugène Delâtre, Latenay, Meunier, Osterlind, Thaulow, and Marie Gautier. He was, however, thrifty in his extravagance, preferring to purchase the ordinary impression of *Dance of Light* by Osterlind (80 francs) rather than an impression with *remarque* (100 francs).[9] Etchings exhibited at other Salons included, in 1908, *The Milliner* by Pierre Gatier (edition of fifty, 30 francs) and eight etchings by Michl; in 1909, *Time to Rest* by Boutet de Monvel (edition of sixty, 60 francs) and *Factories in the Snow* by Raffaëlli (edition on Japanese imperial paper, 100 francs); in 1910, *Breakfast*, also by Raffaëlli (edition of thirty, 200 francs) and *La Clavelito* by Detouche (edition of fifty, 30 francs). But already, the success of the Salons was resulting in a significant decrease in the quality of the work exhibited.

Their success also brought societies from other countries to France. The first exhibition of the English Society of Etchers was held in November-December 1910 at the Manzi and Joyant gallery (15 rue de la Ville-L'Évêque). All of Roussel's color etchings were shown, including *Last Poppies, A Window Seen through a Window, Anemones, Summer,* and *Chelsea Palaces.*

47a

Dancer,
c. 1904
Charles Cottet

47b

Dancer,
c. 1904
Charles Cottet

168

Spring,
n.d.
Manuel Robbe

154

*The Englishman at
the Folies-Bergère,*
1899
Richard Ranft

153

In the Box,
c. 1899
Richard Ranft

RICHARD RANFT

157

Polo,
c. 1900
Richard Ranft

Épreuve d'artiste   Richard Roux   no3302

L'heure du repos. tiré. 60.10

7

BERNARD R. DE MONTZ

H. Detouche

Henry Detouche   La Clavelito dans El Garrotin —   5-60

Robbe — le choix de l'Épreuve

tirée à 50 Épreuves

Imprimerie Delâtre

COLOR ETCHING AT THE SALON

Artists also strove to exhibit their color etchings at the official annual Salon. In 1890, the Salon was disrupted: the Société des Artistes Français held the traditional May 1 Salon, presided by William-Adolphe Bouguereau, in the Palais de l'Industrie on the Champs-Elysées, but dissident artists, led by Meissonier, formed the Société Nationale des Beaux-Arts and exhibited their work on the Champ-de-Mars on May 15. The alternative Salon was not, in fact, particularly revolutionary, yet color etching was nevertheless represented at the beginning, in 1890, by Guérard's *Peach and Grapes*. The 1893 exhibition included Bracquemond's *The Rainbow*, Delâtre's *In a Garden*, and Guérard's *A Pontoon, Venice*. Houdard showed *Frogs and Reeds* and Cap-

ucines in 1895. Other works exhibited included, in 1899, Robbe's *Choosing the Proof* and Villon's *Sulking* and *Hey, Class*; in 1902, his *Bibi la Purée* and *Little Mother*; in 1903, Chahine's *A Hold*; and in 1904, Ranft's *Haystacks in the Snow*, published by Pierrefort.

Artists also exhibited at the Salon d'Automne (Boutet, Jourdain, Müller, Ranft, and Taquoy were included in the 1904 Salon) and at the Salon des Artistes Indépendants at Cours-la-Reine. Among the six thousand works exhibited in 1910, Guillaume Apollinaire noted that "the color etchings by Mlle. Krouglikoff are among the most beautiful contemporary work we have."[10]

Yet that same year he refused to give a detailed account of "French artists, whose primary characteristic, above all, is artistic honesty." He continued: "This quality is very important, but it can not replace the others. Most of these artists are behind the times; although almost all of them have learned the rudiments of their art, they seem to be ignorant of life itself and the beauty of works exhibited in museums . . . and this creates sincere people, talented in their fields, who are usually condemned to perpetual mediocrity."[11] Apollinaire cited only one name, an artist unknown today, "M. Coraboeuf, who is talented [and who is] also a brilliant color etcher." His criticism continued: "Everything that is not sculpture or painting is somewhat sacrificed at the Salon of the Société des Artistes Français. In fact, it is merely a jumbled collection of pastels, miniatures and etchings."[12]

Finally color etchings appeared at the Universal Expositions. On the occasion of the decennial, Gustave Coquiot wrote in *La Plume* (August 1, 1900), "color etching is represented by Georges Jeanniot; polychrome etchings that humorously illustrate *Polo* or *The National Service Examination*." He also wrote that "the original drypoints by J. F. Raffaëlli—*Two Friends, Narrow Street, Road with Tall Trees, Les Invalides* and *The Actress*—demonstrate marvelously the talent and knowledge of this admirable painter. This is unquestionably a confident master with an original grasp of color and an unequaled ability to

Dis donc, mon p'tit, va fallait te trotter ; t'as pas l'air
de te douter que le conseil des ministres est à dix heures...

*The Wrestlers:
A Hold,*
1902
Edgar Chahine
(Detail on
facing page)

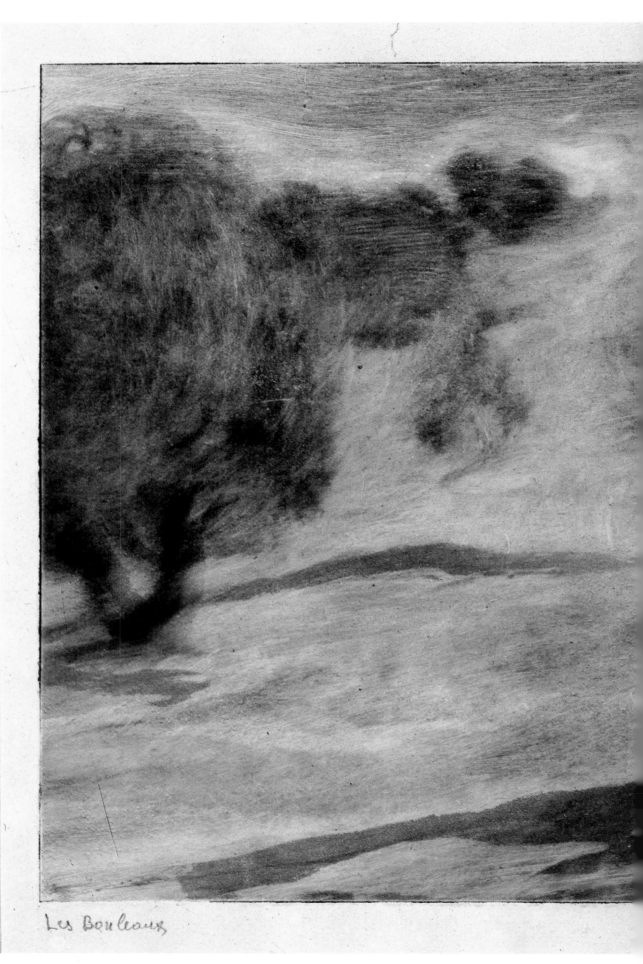

Les Bouleaux

105

The Silver Birches,
c. 1902
**Elisabeth
Krouglicoff**

E. Kroughicoff

100

Polo,
c. 1900

Georges Jeanniot
(Detail on
facing page)

situate the human figure in a scene. What intimacy and what philosophy, so peaceful and familiar!"

THE ROLE OF THE STATE

The government remained strangely removed from the gradual but steady development of color etching in France. Experimental, artistic etchings were of no interest to the state, which began to play a part only when commercial engravings had flooded the market.

Three facts corroborate this. Copyright law had applied to prints since the seventeenth century. Publishers and printers were required to deposit three or four copies of each of the images put up for sale, in application of articles 3 and 4 of the law of July 29, 1881. The records of the copyright offices are therefore good sources, revealing the extent of the

printing production. For each print, they specifically indicate the name of the depositor, the author of the work, the title, the technique, and the size of the edition. An examination of the records corresponding to the years 1877 to 1912 (kept in the National Archives and provided by the Ministry of the Interior) reveals that a large majority of the production consisted of lithographic prints, which were gradually replaced by color lithography, then by photography.[13] Etchings, especially color etchings, appear only rarely until 1888, and then only as color reproductions of paintings; the copyrights sometimes even refer to a second edition of an old plate. On April 7, 1877, Goupil copyrighted *Education of a Young Girl*, engraved by Hester after Goubie; on August 21, 1886, Geny-Gros reprinted *Madness*, engraved by Janinet after Fragonard (edition of fifty) and again reprinted an edition of 100

impressions of *Love* on November 14, 1888 (the original is dated 1777).

Color etchings appeared more regularly after 1888. Laurent, Wittmann, Geny-Gros and, especially, Boussod-Valadon regularly copyrighted etchings destined for a large public, as indicated by the large editions—of 150 to 1,100 (*Zaïrette*, copyrighted by Geny-Gros on July 10, 1893)—but actually these were made using the photorelief color printing process, chromophotogravure. Étienne Boussod (son-in-law of the print dealer Adolphe Goupil) and Valadon, installed at 2 Place de l'Opéra, 9 rue Chaptal (print shop), 10 boulevard Montparnasse, and later boulevard des Capucines, created Boussod, Manzi, Joyant in 1888. They specialized in facsimile copies of watercolors or miniatures, which contributed a great deal to promoting the popularity of color etchings. Examples of their production include *Le Fil de la Vierge* by Boichard, *The Swing* by Flameng, *The Tyrolean* by Rossi, and *Pointing at Woodcock* by Gélibert. On February 5, 1888, a color album by Boutet, *Around Them*, was copyrighted by Chamerot and Renouard.

In 1903 the term "color etching" was finally mentioned, but it still referred to engravings reproducing other works of art, such as *Morning, Italian Souvenir*, engraved by Brouet after Corot

(edition of 150 by Pierrefort), and *Portrait of the Mother of the Artist Whistler*, copyrighted by Geny-Gros in April 1905 (edition of 300 printed by Piazza et Cie.).

However dealers were beginning to copyright limited editions of original color etchings by artists. On August 3, 1903, Sagot copyrighted *Gust of Wind, Place Saint-Germain-L'Auxerrois* by Bertrand and *Path at Hyde Park* by Müller, an edition of fifty printed by Eugène Delâtre. On March 31, 1908, Robert Arnot copyrighted *Before the Storm* by Eugène Delâtre and on June 7, 1910, Manzi copyrighted *Portrait of a Woman* by Helleu (edition of 150).

The records for print distribution kept by the Direction des Beaux-Arts corroborate this slow acceptance of color etching.[14] Before World War I, the only entry is Buhot's series, *Japonisme, Ten Etchings* of which only twelve copies were distributed from February 1889 to 1891, an insignificant number compared to the great number of lithographs offered to societies and museums. Not until after the war did Armand Coussens (1881-1935), a specialist in color softground and drypoint etchings, manage to obtain a quasi-monopoly for these official distributions.

The records for etchings in the Print and Photography Department of the Bibliothèque Nationale show that this institution was also lagging behind: *Choosing the Proof* by Manuel Robbe is the only copyrighted print. As a reflection of

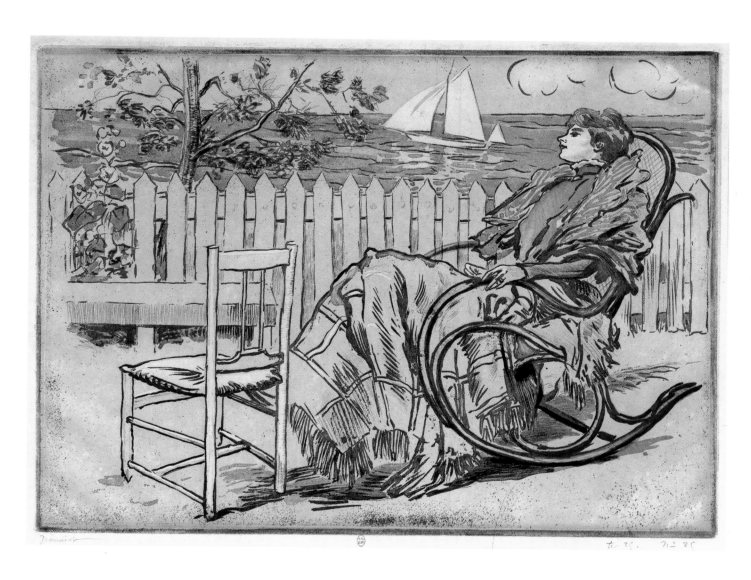

the weak interest in color etchings, acquisitions were virtually nonexistent before World War I. On June 14, 1913, *To the Glory of the Cat* by Detouche was purchased from Loÿs Delteil, author of *Peintre Graveur illustré*, who was, in fact, opposed to color etching.

Very few prints were acquired between the two world wars. Among these were four etchings by Mary Cassatt: one purchased from M. Stölin in 1921 (*In the Omnibus*), two from Marcel Guiot (*The Fitting* and *Mother's Kiss*), and one at an auction in Zurich of the Laffon collection in 1938 (*The Banjo Lesson*). Two etchings by Jeanniot were purchased from the artist in 1933: *Woman in a Rocking Chair* and *On the Beach*. And finally, *La Soupeuse* by Bottini was purchased

from Paul Prouté in 1939. A few prints were bought at auctions during and after the war. *The Pond* by Cassatt was acquired in 1947, and *Un Couple de Soupeuses* by Chahine in 1984. A few rare prints were purchased from artists (*Spanish Dancer* was purchased from Villon in 1950) or from Parisian dealers to complete the Impressionist collection in the Print Department. Three etchings by Raffaëlli were bought in 1942 from Paul Prouté (*The Actress, Gentleman Having Just Painted His Gate,* and *The Little Milliner*); and *In the Wheatfields* by Guérard was acquired from Prouté in 1953. Three etchings by Delâtre were bought: two from Mme. Maurice Le Garrec (*Landscape* and *Night* in 1942) and one from Henri Petiet (*The Dressmaker* in 1942). Finally,

101

Woman in a Rocking Chair, 1900

Georges Jeanniot

On the Beach,
c. 1900
Georges Jeanniot

63

The Dressmaker,
c. 1894
Eugène Delâtre

152

The Little Milliner,
n.d.
Jean-François Raffaëlli

Negro Made Good by Villon was purchased from Le Garrec in 1949.

Fortunately, donations compensated for the lack of foresight on the part of the government, which often lagged fifty years behind the times, deciding to purchase an artist's work long after it was too late. Until World War I, donations were made by the artists themselves: Charles Houdard offered *End of Day* in 1908; Chahine, *The Terrace, The Wrestlers: A Hold* and *The Streetwalkers* in 1908; and Villon, *Society Comedy, The Cards, Women of Ouessant* and *Sulking* in 1912.

Even dealers occasionally donated works: Hessèle gave Houdard's *Capucines* on May 29, 1899; the Print Department thereby acquired an impression that was different from the copyrighted print dated June 10, 1898. On February 18, 1901 Pierrefort donated three etchings by Robbe (*The Love Letter, Woman on a Chaise Longue,* and *The Harvesters*) and four by Sunyer (*At the Luxembourg Gardens, The Shoelace Seller, The Ragpicker,* and *At the Puppet Show*).

Steinlein   Les Promeneuses

167

The Love Letter,
n.d.
Manuel Robbe

46

The Streetwalkers,
1907
Edgar Chahine

43

Un Couple
de Soupeuses,
1901
Edgar Chahine

42

The Terrace,
1899
Edgar Chahine

96
Capucines,
c. 1895
Charles-Louis
Houdard

166
The Harvesters,
n.d.
Manuel Robbe

190

*At the Luxembourg
Gardens,*
c. 1900
Joaquin Sunyer y Miro

192

At the Puppet Show,
c. 1900
Joaquin Sunyer y Miro

After 1918, families of several artists donated works in memory of a relative: Auguste Delâtre, Jean Guérard, Pissarro's children, Raffaëlli's daughter: Madame Chevrier de Beauchesne, Helleu's daughter: Madame Howard Johnston, Georges-Henri Rivière, and Madame Marcel Duchamp.

Collectors also donated their prints. *Portrait of Auguste Delâtre* by his son Eugène was given by Béjot on March 9, 1933. *Songs of Bilitis* by Marie Laurencin was donated by Seymour de Ricci on January 6, 1936. Atherton Curtis donated part of his priceless collection on October 26, 1949, including *The Wagoners, Theater Corridor, Cakewalk, Reclining Woman* and *Supper*, by Bottini; *Portrait of Madeleine Cartier* by Helleu; *The Seine at Asnières* and *Factories in the Snow* by Raffaëlli; *Flessingue* by Signac; and *The Washerwomen* and *Reclining Nude* by Steinlen.

The final method of acquisition available to the Print Department was buying from museums. Arrangements were made whereby the Bibliothèque Nationale received prints—for conservation—from modern art museums as they renewed their collections. On April 2, 1931, the Musée Luxembourg gave color etchings by Boutet de Monvel, Bruyer, Cottet, Eugène Delâtre, Jourdain, Pissarro, Raffaëlli,

99

The Outdoor Concert,
c. 1900
Francisco Iturrino

1906

Marie Laurencin
Les chansons de Bilitis

106

The Songs of Bilitis,
1906

Marie Laurencin

Ranft, Rivière, and Villon to the Bibliothèque Nationale.

This was due in particular to Léonce Bénédite, who took up Philippe Burty's idea of creating a print department at the museum. In a note of April 15, 1890, he suggested that "after the death of the artist, the prints would go to the Bibliothèque Nationale, which is now overburdened by donations of badly kept material."[15] Between 1904 and 1911 the state acquired 150 prints at the Salons of the Société de la Gravure Originale en Couleurs, and these were then passed to the Print Department.[16] Donations by the curators of the Musée de Luxembourg meant that the state acquired some exceptional works, such as *Dusk with Haystacks* by Pissarro, at relatively low prices. On July 5, 1963 seven color etchings by Mary Cassatt were transferred from the Musée d'Art Moderne to the Bibliothèque Nationale.

6

The Wagoners,
1903
**Georges-Alfred
Bottini**

8

Theater Corridor,
c. 1906
**Georges-Alfred
Bottini**

The Skater,
1905

**Bernard Boutet
de Monvel**

THE TRIUMPH OF COMMERCIAL ETCHING

"The art of etching is more respected than ever before, and the techniques that were supposed to have been so damaging have only served to reveal its artistic merits," wrote Apollinaire in L'Intransigeant (November 13, 1910).[17]

In 1913, Raffaëlli rejoiced that "our ideas have finally prevailed. Original color and black-and-white etchings have triumphed, particularly color etching. Numerous exhibitions demonstrate this every day, and a legion of collectors support us. A publishers' survey has revealed that during this last decade, sales of prints have exceeded four million francs! We should be happy with this unexpected success and be prepared for many new efforts, which, day by day, will bring us more and more beautiful things!"[18]

That same year, the city of Reims held its second annual Salon of the Société de la Gravure Originale en Couleurs, and most of the Parisian artists participated. Yet the catalogue for the Salon betrays an irreparable decline in the artistic quality of color etching, which had fallen victim to its own popularity. The artists promoted by Georges Petit in this luxuriously illustrated catalogue included Maurice Bompard, Georges François, Julien Celos, Edgar Bouillette, Louis Dauphin, Victor Gilsoul, Paul Girardet, Henri Jourdain, Gaston de Latenay, Le Goût-Gérard, Henri Le Riche, Luigini, Louis Icart, and Rodocanachi.

Works reproduced included *Lake of Love*, *The Mysterious Hour*, *Golden Reflections*, *The Interlude*, *La Frileuse*, and *The Sad Hour*. These works attest to the sentimental quality of turn-of-the-century color etchings. Some artists, such as Robbe, Malo-Renault, the worldly Gatier, or Lepape, still demonstrated a certain elegance and unaffected refinement; but others, Raoul du Gardier and Louis Icart, for example, represented the newer style. The war years accentuated this state of affairs: as predicted by Pissarro, "a bunch of charlatans making insipid, pretty things" began to dominate the print world. "Boudoir etching" prevailed and became, in the 1920s, a typically French product that symbolized Parisian chic. But the era of artistic color etching had come to an end. It would be renewed in Paris again only in the late 1920s by the British printmaker Stanley William Hayter.

51

Sisters of Saint-Esprit around a Coffin,
1906
Charles Cottet

23

Old Man Walking,
1906
Georges Bruyer

NOTES

Introduction

1. A.N., X1a 8653, fol. 83; B.N., Mss., ms. fr. 21732, fol. 138-141.
2. A. Hyatt Mayor, Prints and People, a Social History of Printed Pictures (New York, 1971); and Sue Welsh Reed, article to appear in Nouvelles de l'Estampe.
3. Jeanne Duportal, Étude sur les livres à figures édités en France de 1601 à 1660 (Paris: H. Champion 1914), VIII: 391.
4. Japonisme has been and still is a subject of much research. Sources include: Ives Colta, The Great Wave: The Influence of Japanese Woodcuts on French Prints (New York: Metropolitan Museum of Art, 1974); Siegfried Wichmann, Japonisme, The Japanese Influence on Western Art in the 19th and 20th Centuries (New York: Harmony Books, 1981); Le Japonisme, Galeries nationales du Grand Palais, Paris, May 17-August 15, 1988 (Paris: Éditions de la R.M.N., 1988).
5. Edmond and Jules de Goncourt, Journal, Mémoires de la vie littéraire, III, 1887-96 (Paris: R. Laffont, Collection Bouquins, 1989) 402, 890.
6. Michel Melot and Barbara Stern Shapiro, "Catalogue sommaire des monotypes de Camille Pissarro," Nouvelles de l'Estampe (January-February 1975).
7. Janine Bailly-Herzberg, ed., Correspondance de Camille Pissarro, I, 1865-85, letters 83-84 (Paris: P.U.F., 1980), 140-143.
8. A.N., F18 * I 24, nos. 197, 271 and 279 (registrations of patents and reports from printers and bookstores). Unfortunately, this patent could not be found in the printers' files F18 1853 and F18 1837.
9. Gabriel Mourey, "Coloured Etchings in France," The Studio, XXII, no. 95 (February 1901), 3-14, 94-103.
10. Jean-François Raffaëlli, Préface du catalogue du 10ᵉ Salon annuel de la gravure originale en couleurs, November 1913 (Paris: G. Petit, 1913), 6.

From Pissarro to Picasso: The Revival of Color Etching in France

1. For a discussion on the history of color lithography at the end of the nineteenth century see: Phillip Dennis Cate and Sinclair Hamilton Hitchings, The Color Revolution, Color Lithography in France, 1890-1900 (New Brunswick: The Rutgers University Art Gallery, 1978).
2. An impression of Manet's Boy Blowing Bubble printed by Guérard à la poupée in blue exists in the collection of the Art Institute of Chicago, inventory no. 1921.377.
3. Armond Fields, Henri Rivière (Salt Lake City: Gibbs M. Smith Inc., 1983 and Paris: Éditions Hubschmid & Bouret, 1985), 85, L'Enterrement aux parapluies.
4. Claudie Bertin, Henri Guérard, l'œuvre gravé (Mémoire de l'École du Louvre cours d'histoire de la gravure, 1975), vol. 1, 62.
5. Ibid.
6. Octave Uzanne, "La Gravure en couleur le renouveau de la taille douce polychrome," Le Livre moderne, no. 9 (September 10, 1890), 148-152.
7. Ibid, 152.
8. Loÿs Delteil, J.-F. Raffaëlli, le Peintre-Graveur, vol. 16 (Paris, 1923).
9. "Pan! Pan! Qu'est-ce qu'est là? C'est le portrait frappant de ressemblance du futur président d'un conseil de ministres, en France ou ailleurs." Catalogue illustré de l'Exposition des arts incohérents (Paris: Bernard et Cie, 1884), 41.
10. See Weisberg et al., Japonisme, Japanese Influence on French Art 1854-1910 (Cleveland: The Cleveland Museum of Art, 1975); Siegfried Wichmann, Japonisme; Le Japonisme, catalogue for the exhibition at the Grand Palais, Paris, May 17-August 15, 1988 (Édition de la Réunion des Musées Nationaux, 1988).
11. Introduced to Japan from the West in the first half of the nineteenth century, aniline pigments allowed woodblock artists to print with strong, sometimes garish colors. Rich Prussian blue was favored by Hokusai and Hiroshige for their monochromatic prints.
12. In Spain Picasso created his first etching, El Zurdo (1899), of which only one impression exists today. Five years later in Paris he etched The Frugal Repast upon a used zinc plate which retains the intaglio vestiges of a landscape design. It has been suggested that Picasso's fellow expatriate, Ricardo Canals, had first worked on the plate and, having partially effaced the landscape image, offered it to the impoverished Picasso (see Roger Passeron, Picasso (Paris: Bibliothèque des Arts, 1984), 18. Eugène Delâtre printed thirty proofs of The Frugal Repast in 1904, of which at least two were printed in blue or blue-green. These rare color impressions are in the collections of the Art Institute of Chicago and one is on loan to the National Gallery of Art, Washington, D.C.
13. Sue Welsh Reed and Barbara Stern Shapiro, Edgar Degas: The Painter as Printmaker (Boston: Museum of Fine Arts, 1984), li.
14. Joseph Pennell, Etchers and Etching (New York: The MacMillan Company, 1936), 277.
15. Roger Portalis, "La Gravure en Cou-

leurs," La Gazette des Beaux-Arts (February 1890), 127-128.
16. Cate and Hitchings, 1, 34. This was not the case with the Salon de la Société Nationale des Beaux-Arts, which, as Marianne Grivel's essays indicate, included color etchings beginning in 1893.
17. L'Estampe et l'Affiche, April 1897.
18. I am grateful to Marianne Grivel for providing this information and that covered by note 17.
19. Jules Adeline, Les Arts de reproduction vulgarisés (Paris: May & Motteroz, 1894), 342-343.
20. Janine Bailly-Herzberg, Dictionnaire de l'estampe en France 1830-1950 (Paris: Arts et Métiers Graphiques, 1985), 269; Léon Rosenthal, La Gravure (Paris: Librairie Renouard, 1909), 382.
21. John Rewald, ed., Camille Pissarro: Letters to His Son Lucien (Salt Lake City: Peregrine Smith Inc., 1981), 287.
22. Adelyn D. Breeskin, The Graphic Work of Mary Cassatt, A Catalogue Raisonné (New York: H. Bittner and Co., 1948), cat. nos. 108, 109, 126.
23. Nancy Mowll Mathews and Barbara Stern Shapiro, Mary Cassatt: The Color Prints (New York: Abrams, 1989), 70.
24. Phillip Dennis Cate, Charles Maurin (New York: Lucien Goldschmidt Inc., 1978), 7-8.
25. Barbara Stern Shapiro, Camille Pissarro, The Impressionist Printmaker (Boston: Museum of Fine Arts, 1973), unpaginated, 10 of introduction.
26. Exhibitions of the Society of Printmakers 1889-1897 (New York: Garland Publishing Inc., 1981).
27. For more discussion of these influences on color printmaking see Cate and Hitchings, 1-15.
28. For a discussion of the relationship of printmaking to the Arts and Crafts Movement, see Patricia Eckert Boyer's essay in L'Estampe originale, Artistic Printmaking in France 1893-1895 (Amsterdam: Van Gogh Museum, 1991), 26-45.
29. Delteil, cat. nos. 8-13.
30. The exhibition took place from January 30 to February 11, 1893.
31. For examples of Raffaëlli's color illustrations for Le Paris illustré see issues July 1, 1884, "Les Fêtes foraines," and August 1, 1886, "Les Cafés-concerts." In the July 1893 issue of Le Figaro illustré Lautrec used the photorelief process to illustrate Gustave Geoffroy's article "Le Plaisir à Paris: les restaurants et les cafés-concerts des Champs-Elysées," Les Types de Paris (Paris: Édition Figaro, E. Plon Nourrit et Cie., 1889).
32. For a description and discussion of photo-printing processes at the end of the nineteenth century see Phillip Dennis Cate, "Printing in France, 1850-1900: The Artist and New Technologies," Gazette of the Grolier Club, new series nos. 28/29 (June/December 1978), 57-73.
33. Georges Lecomte, "Les Pointes-Sèches en couleurs de J.-F. Raffaëlli," L'Estampe et L'Affiche, vol. 2 (1898), 218.
34. Delteil, cat. no. 21.

35. Lecomte, 218-219.

36. Ibid, 220.

37. See Phillip Dennis Cate in Weisberg et al., 54-55.

38. Mathews and Shapiro, 62-63.

39. Mathews and Shapiro, 36.

40. Breeskin, cat. nos. 127-138.

41. Mathews and Shapiro, 37.

42. For a visual comparison of Cassatt's *The Tub* to that of Utamaro see Weisberg et al., 91.

43. Mathews and Shapiro, 38.

44. Rewald, 196.

45. Ibid, 204.

46. Ibid, 196.

47. Loÿs Delteil, *Camille Pissarro, le peintre-graveur illustré*, vol. XVII (1923).

48. Rewald, 327.

49. Cate, *Charles Maurin*, 7.

50. For another example of Maurin and Lautrec simultaneously experimenting in the application of color in their work see Cate, *Charles Maurin*, 9.

51. Edmond Sagot sale catalogue no. 34, September 1892, no. 5983 Maurin, no. 5, *"Intérieur de Jardin/Jeune fille cousant sur un banc.* Planche en couleurs à repérages, in-4 en hauteur 10 fr; planche détruite après un tirage de quelques épreuves."

52. For discussions on the revival of etching in France and on the role of Auguste Delâtre see Gabriel Weisberg, *The Etching Renaissance in France, 1850-1880* (Salt Lake City: Utah Museum of Fine Arts, 1971) and Janine Bailly-Hertzberg, *L'Eau-forte de peintre au dix-neuvieme siècle: La Societe des aquafortistes 1862-67* (Paris, 1972). The address of Delâtre's printing press varied from 2 rue Tourlaque to 92 rue Lepic. During the period that the father and son worked together it varied from 87 to 92, 97 and 102 rue Lepic (information provided by Marianne Grivel).

53. A copy of *Portrait of Pauline* is in the collection of the Boston Public Library.

54. Mathews and Shapiro, 83.

55. Ibid, 49.

56. A talented craftsman, Eugène Delâtre was the printer and friend of all of the great etchers of the time, although Pissarro did not like him. On January 28, 1895, he wrote to Lucien that "these impressions are much cleaner than those pulled by that terrible Delâtre, he overdoes it."[Ed. Janine Bailly-Herzberg, *Correspondance de Camille Pissarro*, IV (Paris: P.U.F., 1980), 26]. Always available, even on Sundays, he introduced various artists to color etching, including Edgar Chahine, Pierre Gatier, Francis Jourdain, Manuel Robbe. He printed the works of Boutet de Monvel, Richard Ranft, Théophile-Alexandre Steinlen and undoubtedly those of Jacques Villon and other members of the Société de la Gravure Originale en Couleurs. Letters from Rivière, Willette, Lepère, and Jeanniot attest to the daily exchanges that contributed to making color etching a typically Parisian phenomenon.

"Dear Monsieur Delâtre, at home, looking at my impression of *Vagabond* (the last we pulled), I think that we should add *red* to the file; to the *scarf* tied around the neck so that we only see it under the chin; a *vermilion* that looks a little like [a drawing follows], and what would also be good would be a very light green and yellow in the background trees. If you have not yet pulled the impressions, please make these slight changes and then print ten of them like this! And the hat should be as strong as the jacket! All the best and see you tomorrow," wrote the painter-etcher Henri Evenepoel in November 1899. [*Lettres d'Henri-Jacques-Édouard Evenepoel* (Nice, 3 October 1872-Paris, 27 December 1899), Musée Saint-Denis.]

Some time before 1907 Steinlen wrote: "My dear Delâtre, would you be so kind—as you always are—as to transfer from the first plate to the second one so that I can do the color—as you can see, I made holes to register them—I'm sorry I could not come to say hello to your father and you. I was away for almost five months and have been back three weeks. I haven't even been able to go out, I have so much work piled up. I would be grateful if you could do this for me tomorrow morning. I'll come see you around noon. Thank you and all my best to both of you. Yours, Steinlen." [*Delâtre Correspondence*, Boston Public Library, Print Department. The public library has an exceptional collection of works by Delâtre, including some extremely rare prints. These were donated by Eugène Delâtre's daughter, Zélina, to the curator at the time, Arthur W. Heintzelman, who spent a long time with Delâtre learning how to pull the engravings made during his trip to Paris. We would like to express our gratitude to Sinclair Hitchings and his staff for their efficient and friendly assistance.]

In February 1910, Henri Rivière sent this short note to his neighbor (he lived at 29 boulevard de Clichy): "Wednesday, February 23, 1910 (4 pm). My dear friend, I won't be able to come tomorrow for the printing. Could we postpone this until next week, same day, same time? Will this be alright? All the best, Henri Rivière." [*Delâtre Correspondence*, Boston Public Library, Print Department.] I am grateful to Marianne Grivel for contributing these paragraphs.

57. B. N., Est., Li 243 box 27.

58. Letter from Armand Séguin to Auguste Delâtre, 8 June 1895. Pont-Aven Museum.

59. "Tuesday, 25 June 1895. My dear Delâtre, I would be delighted if we could arrange it as you have indicated. Next Friday I will therefore go see the press around two or three at the latest to give you a bill for 150 francs, which represents the 250 francs for the price of the thing. I send all my best to you and Eugène, whose prints I saw—very curious and interesting. Félicien Rops, 2 rue du marché des Blancs-Manteaux." Boston Public Library, Print Department.

60. *Camille Pissarro*, III, letter 974 (2 Jan. 1894) and 978 (14 Jan. 1894) and IV, letter 1618 (17 Jan. 1894), p. 533.

61. I am grateful to Marianne Grivel for this information and for contributing the text covered by notes 57 through 60.

62. Rosenthal, 383.

63. Pennell, 278.

64. Patricia Eckert Boyer and Phillip Dennis Cate, *L'Estampe originale, Artistic Printmaking in France 1893-95* (Amsterdam: Van Gogh Museum, 1991). This publication serves as a *catalogue raisonné* of *L'Estampe originale*.

65. Mathews and Shapiro, 39, 81.

66. Cate and Hitchings, 29.

67. The printer Auguste Clot overstepped the bounds of his craft a number of times and made color lithographic copies after pastels or other media by such artists as Cézanne, Luce and Sisley. See Cate and Hitchings, 26.

68. André Mellerio, "La Lithographie originale en couleurs," *L'Estampe et L'Affiche* (Paris: 1898); for a reprint and English translation of Mellerio's essay see Cate and Hitchings, 77-99.

69. Gabriel Mourey, "Colored Etchings in France," *The Studio*, XXII, no. 95 (February 1901), 3-14, and no. 96 (March 1901), 94-103.

70. Mourey, 103.

71. Oddly, the one great omission of Mourey's overview is Mary Cassatt. He does refer to the work of Marie Gautier, which leads one to believe that the lacuna is not completely based on sexism, and he also discusses the work of the Swiss artist Richard Ranft in depth, suggesting that he was not inclined toward the national chauvinism practiced by the Société des Peintres-Graveurs. Mourey was so perceptive of the virtues of the medium and so up-to-date on the artists working in color etching that it is surprising that he was either ignorant of or not receptive to Cassatt's work. A possible explanation for this gap, however, may be the author's strong reliance on the dealer Charles Hessèle for the article's source material. Mourey accredited Hessèle for the loan of all works illustrated: it is likely that the publisher and dealer also supplied Mourey with a ten-year history of color etching with a bias toward those artists he carried. Cassatt was not one of them.

72. For the Barcelona background of these artists see Marilyn McCully, *El Quatre Gats, Art in Barcelona around 1900* (Princeton: The Art Museum, Princeton University, 1978).

73. Anthony Blunt and Phoebe Pool, *Picasso: The Formative Years* (London: Studio Books, 1962); John Richardson, *A Life of Picasso*, vol. 1 (1881-1906) (New York: Random House, 1991), 173.

74. Jehan Rictus, *Les Soliloques du pauvre, en vente au cabaret des Quat'-z-Arts et chez les libraires*, cover illustration by Steinlen (December 1896), and expanded edition with portraits by Steinlen on cover and frontispiece, dated December 1, 1895 (published by Rictus in 1897); see Théophile Briant, *Jehan Rictus* (Paris: Editions Seghers, 1973), 201; *Les Soliloques du pauvre de Jehan Rictus, suite de huit lithographies en couleurs de Sunyer* (Paris: Pierre Duffau, 1897).

75. "Shit! here is winter in all its harshness . . ." Rictus's "L'Hiver" was written in 1894-95. Yet on December 9, 1896, three nights before Rictus's recital at Quat'-z-Arts cabaret, Alfred Jarry presented the dress rehearsal of *Ubu roi* at the Nouveau Théâtre before an invited audience who were shocked to hear, for the first time, the word "merde" used in a public performance.

76. Phillip Dennis Cate, *The Graphic Arts and French Society, 1871-1914* (New Brunswick: Rutgers University Press, 1988), 25, 43.

77. Marcel Legay (1851-1915) performed songs of social concern by himself and others such as Aristide Bruant at cabarets throughout Paris, beginning at Le Chat Noir in the early 1880s. He also is famous for putting to music the prose of Victor Hugo, Guy de Maupassant, Jean Richipin, and the Communard Louise Michel. At the end of the century he performed regularly at the Quat'-z-Arts and various other cabarets.

78. For a discussion on lithographic albums in France at the end of the century see Phillip Dennis Cate, "From Redon to Rivière: Albums of the 1890s," in Pat Gilmour, ed., *Lasting Impressions, Lithography as Art* (Canberra: Australian National Gallery, 1988), 110-128.

79. Barbara Stern Shapiro also makes this point in *Camille Pissarro 1830-1903*, catalogue for the exhibition held at the Hayward Gallery, London (October 30, 1980-January 11, 1981), the Grand Palais, Paris (January 30-April 27, 1981), and the Museum of Fine Arts, Boston (May 19-August 9, 1981) (Paris: Édition de la réunion des musées nationaux, 1981), entries nos. 164-168, 205-206.

The Expansion of Color Etching in Paris

1. Janine Bailly-Herzberg, ed., *Correspondance de Camille Pissarro*, IV (Paris: P.U.F., 1980), 44-45.

2. Ibid, 223.

3. Ibid, 231.

4. Ibid, 242-243.

5. Ibid, 148-149.

6. Ibid, 76. On Bing, see the pioneering study by Gabriel P. Weisberg, *Art Nouveau Bing: Paris Style 1900* (New York: Abrams, 1986).

7. Edmond and Jules de Goncourt, *Journal, Mémoires de la vie littéraire*, III, 1887-96 (Paris: R. Laffont, Collection Bouquins, 1989), 1266.

8. Jean-François Raffaëlli, *Préface du catalogue du 10e Salon annuel de la gravure originale en couleurs*, November 1913 (Paris: G. Petit, 1913), 7.

9. See the annotated catalogues at the Bibliothèque d'Art et Archéologie Jacques Doucet, Paris.

10. Guillaume Appollinaire, *Chroniques d'art 1902-18*. Texts compiled by L.-C. Breunig (Paris: Gallimard, 1981), 103.

11. Ibid, 125.

12. Ibid, 137.

13. A. N., F18 * VI 82 to 92 10.

14. A. N., F21 7086 to 7089.

15. Anne Distel, "Un achat par l'état d'estampes de Camille Pissarro en 1890 et les débuts d'un Cabinet des estampes au Musée du Luxembourg," *Nouvelles de l'Estampe*, no. 74 (March-April 1894) 8-13.

16. This figure is indicated at the end of the *Catalogue général des eaux-fortes et gravures originales en couleurs publiées par Georges Petit* (Paris: August 1911), 56.

17. Apollinaire, 164.

18. Raffaëlli, 8.

BIOGRAPHIES AND LIST OF WORKS

A brief biography, followed by a list of works included in the exhibition, is included for each artist. At the end of the biography the artist's catalogue raisonné (if available) is given.

A code in parentheses following the title and date of the print refers to the artist's catalogue raisonné; "IFF" refers to the Inventaire du fonds français après 1800, published by the Print Department of the Bibliothèque Nationale; a roman numeral denotes the state of the print, if known.

An asterisk indicates that a print is colored à la poupée from one plate; otherwise each work is produced from more than one plate au repérage, or printed in one color from one plate as indicated.

The abbreviations "ll," "lr" etc. indicate "lower left," "lower right" etc.; "monogram M.N." refers to the monogram of the Musée du Luxembourg, 1899a.

Eugène BÉJOT (1867-1931)
Eugène Béjot studied at the Académie Julian where he met the prolific printmaker-illustrator, Henri Gabriel Ibels (1867-1936). In Spring 1891, Ibels introduced Béjot to etching; over the next forty years Béjot executed 420 prints in various intaglio processes—drypoint, softground, aquatint—mostly printed in black and white and featuring the city of Paris. In 1897 Béjot met Raffaëlli, Bracquemond, and Lepère, all of whom had worked in the process of color etching. In 1898 Béjot printed *The Pont Marie* (L 148) in color from three plates to create the cover for *Entr'actes de pierres* by Maurice Guillemot (published by Henri Floury in 1899); the ten black-and-white etched illustrations inside were also by Béjot. *The Quay of the Hôtel de Ville* and *Between Paris and Charenton*, both of 1899 and printed from four plates, were followed in 1900 by *The Landing Stage* (L 174) and *The City* (L 175). With economic application of local color by means of line etching and aquatint and the infusion of light by the paper itself, he created delicate, realist views of Paris which are comparable to work by Raffaëlli and which complement the more impressionistic, but equally subtle, pastoral landscapes of Pissarro. P. D. C.
[J. Laran, *L'Œuvre Gravé d'Eugène Béjot* (Paris, 1937)]

1 *The Quay of the Hôtel de Ville*
Le Quai de l'Hôtel de Ville, 1899 (L 163)
Etching, 13 x 17.8 cm
Signed: lr in plate "Eug. Béjot Paris '99," ll in pencil "Eug. Béjot," lr in pencil "T à ép. 9"
(Reproduced in G. Mourey, "Coloured Etchings in France," *The Studio*, XXII, 1901)
Zimmerli Art Museum, David A. and Mildred H. Morse Art Acquisition Fund.

2 *Between Paris and Charenton*
Entre Paris et Charenton, 1899 (L 164)
Etching and aquatint, 14.5 x 22 cm
Signed: ll in plate "Eug. Béjot Paris '99," lr in pencil "Eug. Béjot," ll in pencil "T à ép. 15"
Zimmerli Art Museum, David A. and Mildred H. Morse Art Acquisition Fund.

Clément BÉTOUT (dates unknown)
Clément Bétout exhibited with Eugène Delâtre in 1897 and probably received his technical training in printing *au repérage* from the latter. The Zimmerli's series of progressive proofs for *The Wrestlers* demonstrates the systematic process by which Bétout built his composition from a simple black-and-white line etching to an overly elaborate, tonal image with aquatint producing local texture and color. Like Bracquemond and various other turn-of-the-century artists not included in this exhibition, Bétout often went too far, by today's standards, with the reproductive capabilities of the technique. He looked to color etching as a means of producing a facsimile of what he found in nature rather than a creative process to be exploited for its own aesthetic ends. P. D. C.

3a *The Wrestlers*
Les Lutteurs, 1899 (III)
*Aquatint, 27.3 x 36.2 cm
Signed: ll in pencil "Bétout," "3e état no. 5"

Zimmerli Art Museum, David A. and Mildred H. Morse Art Acquisition Fund.

3b The Wrestlers
Les Lutteurs, 1899 (final state)
*Aquatint, 27.3 x 36.5 cm
Signed: ll in plate "Bétout," ll collector's monogram, lr Sagot monogram, lr in blue crayon "Bétout," ll in blue crayon "1ʳᵉ épreuve après l'aciérage"
Zimmerli Art Museum, David A. and Mildred H. Morse Art Acquisition Fund.

Georges-Alfred BOTTINI (1874-1907)

Bottini was born, studied, practiced his art, and lived his entire short life in or around Montmartre. Often compared with Toulouse-Lautrec because of similarities in the subject matter of their art and their dissolute lifestyles, Bottini did, in fact, associate with Lautrec's cabaret milieu of artists and writers. In 1896 and 1897 Harry van der Zee translated nine of Bottini's watercolor designs into the medium of color woodblock, but Bottini himself produced only three color lithographs (including one promoting the printshop of his publisher and dealer Edmond Sagot) and a total of seven known color etchings. Nevertheless, these small but powerful etchings, mostly depicting life in bars and brothels, display a manipulation of technique and image that expresses a spirit of *fin-de-siècle* decadence similar to that of Villon and Sunyer. Working *à la poupée* and leaving smears of dark pigment on the surface of his plate, Bottini created prints which are a hybrid of color etching and monotype; brusquely wiped surface pigments, dabs of color, and figures defined by sketchily etched lines evoke an insubstantial society in which life is wasted or demeaned. P. D. C.
[Edna Carter Southard, *Georges Bottini* (Oxford, Ohio: Miami University Art Museum, 1984)]

4 Reclining Woman
Femme couchée, 1898 (IV)
*Etching and aquatint, 19 x 27.9 cm
Signed: lr in pencil "Georges Bottini 98"
Bibliothèque Nationale, D. 7374 (legs A. Curtis no. 539); Dc 597.

5 The Cakewalk
Le Cake-walk, 1903
Etching and softground, 16.9 x 21.2 cm
Signed: lr in pencil "Georges Bottini 1903," ll "7/40"
Bibliothèque Nationale, D. 7374 (legs A. Curtis no. 538); Dc 597.

6 The Wagoners
Les Rouliers, 1903
Etching and softground, 15 x 21.7 cm
Signed: lr in pencil "Georges Bottini 1903"
Bibliothèque Nationale, D. 7374 (legs A. Curtis no. 535); Dc 597.

7 La Soupeuse, 1903 (IFF 2)
Etching and softground, 18 x 20.7 cm
Signed: lr in pencil "Georges Bottini 1903," lc "La Soupeuse," ll "10/40"
Bibliothèque Nationale, A. 9491 (Paul Prouté, 10 March 1939); Dc 597.

8 Theater Corridor
Couloir de théâtre, c. 1906
Etching and softground, 20.7 x 14.4 cm
Signed: lr in pencil "Couloir de théâtre tiré à 40/Georges Bottini"
Bibliothèque Nationale, D. 7374 (legs A. Curtis no. 537); Dc 597.

9 Boxing Match
Match de Boxe, n.d.
Etching and softground, 16.5 x 24 cm
Signed: (verso) lithograph in green of two nude women on a beach by F. Launay, inscribed in pencil "à l'ami Bottini F. Launay"
Zimmerli Art Museum, David A. and Mildred H. Morse Art Acquisition Fund.

10 Supper
Le Souper ou Cabinet Particulier, n.d.
Etching and softground, 20 x 40 cm
Bibliothèque Nationale, D. 7374 (legs A. Curtis no. 542); Dc 597.

Henri BOUTET (1851-1919)

An illustrator and printmaker who specialized in drypoint and etching, Boutet also was actively involved with a group of artists and writers, Les Incohérents (1882-95). By 1888 he was regarded as an established creative printmaker: he was represented in Auguste Lepère's L'Estampe Originale albums of 1888 and 1889 and in André Marty's reworked and more avant-garde version of L'Estampe Originale of 1893. In the 1880s Boutet published a treatise for amateurs entitled La Gravure à l'eau-forte simplifiée par Henri Boutet and a monthly review entitled L'Eau-Forte. His typical drypoint subject was that of the "petit-trottin," a pretty young girl of ambiguous social position. During the 1890s he concentrated on Parisian women of various social classes and this resulted in numerous small publications illustrated with one-color etchings, as well as some large-format caricatures produced *au repérage*. P. D. C.

11 Dis donc, mon p'tit..., c. 1895
Etching and softground, 40.2 x 28.8 cm
Signed: lr in plate "Henri Boutet," lr in pencil "50/15 Henri Boutet," lr artist's monogram, lc inscription in plate "Dis donc, mon p'tit, va falloir te trotter; t'as pas l'air de te douter que le conseil des ministres est à dix heures. ...."
Zimmerli Art Museum, gift of Mr. and Mrs. Herbert Littman.

12 Oui, Monsieur le Comte..., c. 1895
Etching and softground, 40.8 x 28.8 cm
Signed: lr in plate "Henri Boutet," lr in pencil 50/15 Henri Boutet," lr artist's monogram, inscription lc in plate "Oui, Monsieur le Comte, 76 ans! Et il vient ici trois fois par semaine. ...."
Zimmerli Art Museum, gift of Mr. and Mrs. Herbert Littman.

13 Plaisir d'amour..., c.1895
Etching and aquatint, 40.6 x 28.7 cm
Signed: lr artist's monogram, lr in pencil "Épreuve d'État," lc inscription in image in pencil "Plaisir d'amour ne dure qu'un moment. Chagrin d'amour dure toute la vie. (air connu) Henri Boutet"
Zimmerli Art Museum, gift of Mr. and Mrs. Herbert Littman.

Bernard BOUTET DE MONVEL (1884-1949)

Son of painter-etcher Maurice Boutet de Monvel and a pupil of Luc-Olivier Merson and Jean Dampt, Bernard Boutet de Monvel exhibited his work at the Salon from 1902. He produced about a hundred stylized and refined color etchings, often featuring Balzac's Lions and the elegant figures of the Directory period. Besides these evocations of the *demi-monde*, he also depicted more popular subjects (The Beggars, The Tramps) and landscapes. He was present at the Salon of the Société de la Gravure Originale en Couleurs from 1904, when he exhibited eighteen etchings, including The Bar, The Skater, and The Haulers. He also participated at this Salon in 1905 (Skating), in 1907 (The Lioness, The Easy Woman), in 1909 (Time to Rest), in 1911 (The Hydrangeas), and after the war in 1920. He printed with Eugène Delâtre. Starting with editions of twenty-five (The Young Man), Boutet de Monvel increased his print runs to sixty or one hundred as his work became commercially successful. From 1912 he also contributed to the Gazette du Bon Ton. M. G.

14 Brittany Peasant Woman
Paysanne bretonne, 1900
Etching and aquatint, 44.2 x 23.9 cm
Signed: ll in plate in reverse "Bernard B. de Monvel 1900," lr in pencil "Bernard B. de Monvel"
Zimmerli Art Museum, David A. and Mildred H. Morse Art Acquisition Fund.

15 Old Man Sitting
Viel Homme assis, c. 1900
Etching and aquatint touched with gouache, 33 x 27.2 cm
Signed: lr in plate in reverse "Bernard B. de Monvel"
(Reproduced in G. Mourey, "Colored Etchings in France," The Studio, XXII, 1901)
Zimmerli Art Museum, David A. and Mildred H. Morse Acquisition Fund.

16 The Bar
Le Bar, 1901 (IFF 1)
Etching and aquatint, 49.7 x 20.5 cm
Signed: ll in plate in reverse and under the borderline in pencil "Bernard B. de Monvel," lc in pencil "Le Bar—tiré a 30/29," lr monogram M.N.
Bibliothèque Nationale, D. 3302 (Musée du Luxembourg, 2 April 1931); Dc 366.

17 Reaper
Faucheur, 1901 (IFF 1)
Etching and aquatint, 42.2 x 19.4 cm
Signed: ll in plate in reverse, ll in pencil "Bernard B. de Monvel—tiré à 30/4," lr "1901—25 (francs?)," lc "Faucheur"
Bibliothèque Nationale, D. 4671 (M. Bernard Boutet de Monvel, 29 December 1938); Dc 366.

18 Man with Dog
L'Homme au chien, 1905
Etching and aquatint, 43.5 x 34.5 cm
Signed: ll in plate in reverse "Bernard B. de Monvel 1905," ll in pencil within plate mark "Bernard B. de Monvel," ll in pencil "L'Homme au chien—état"
Zimmerli Art Museum, Class of 1937 Art Purchase Fund.

19 *The Skater*
La Patineuse, 1905
Etching and aquatint , 30.1 x 26.5 cm
Signed: ll in plate in reverse "Bernard B. de Monvel 1905," lr in pencil "Bernard B. de Monvel," ll in pencil "La Patineuse tiré à 50/37"
Zimmerli Art Museum, Lillian Lilien Memorial Fund.

20 *Time to Rest*
L'Heure du Repos, c. 1909 (IFF 5)
Etching and aquatint, 36 x 33.8 cm
Signed: lr in plate monogram BM, lr in pencil "Bernard B. de Monvel," ll "L'heure du repos—tiré à 60/10"
Bibliothèque Nationale, D. 3302 (Musée du Luxembourg, 2 April 1931); Dc 366.

Félix BRACQUEMOND (1833-1914)

Painter-etcher, ceramist, and writer, Félix Bracquemond was a pioneer in the renaissance of color etching. Beginning at the age of fifteen as an apprentice to a lithographic printer, he learned his profession by studying the work of Jean-Jacques de Boisseau, Charles Jacque, Eugène Blery, and Louis Marvy. He produced his first etching in 1843, but his fame as an etcher dates from the 1855 Salon at which he exhibited *Top Panel of a Door* (1852), *Sarcelles* (1853), and *Margot la Pie* (1853). These plates were printed by Auguste Delâtre. In 1856 he acquired his own press and began to pull trial proofs himself. From 1862 to 1867 he was involved with the Société des Aquafortistes and etched several plates for the society. In 1873 he produced *Au Jardin d'Acclimatation*, an etching and aquatint printed *au repérage* from four plates. In 1893 he began to etch *The Rainbow*, published by Edmond Sagot in March 1897; this etching was printed in an edition of twenty-five but the plates were canceled. According to *L'Estampe et l'Affiche*, he made "attempts at printing in color *au repérage* using new combinations of processes, resulting in many different, and consequently unique, prints; their price varies from 50 to 200 francs." In the 1904 Salon of the Société de la Gravure Originale en Couleurs, he exhibited *Bather* (edition of sixty, plate not canceled). Made Chevalier de la Légion d'Honneur in 1882, Bracquemond was a well-known painter-etcher and played an important role in artistic society at the turn of the century. M. G.

21 *Au Jardin d'Acclimatation*, 1873 (IFF 343—VII)
Etching and aquatint, 21.2 x 22 cm
Bibliothèque Nationale, B. 214; Ef 411, t. X.

22a *The Rainbow*
L'Arc-en-ciel, 1893 (IFF 446)
Black-and-white etching with watercolor, 41 x 54 cm
Signed: lr "B" monogram
Zimmerli Art Museum, Friends Purchase Fund.

22b *The Rainbow*
L'Arc-en-ciel, 1893 (IFF 446)
Etching and lithograph in color, 41 x 54 cm
Signed: lr "B," lr in plate "1893"
Zimmerli Art Museum, Friends Purchase Fund.

Georges-Léon BRUYER (1883-?)

Grandson of Léon Bruyer, Georges-Léon Bruyer was a pupil of Jean-Léon Gérôme and Gabriel Ferrier at the École des Beaux Arts. In the tradition of Toulouse-Lautrec, his first works comprised color aquatints and powerful etchings. After World War I he produced color woodblocks and etchings featuring the life around Les Halles and worked for various reviews. He exhibited etchings at the Salon d'Automne from 1906, at the Salon of the Société Nationale des Beaux-Arts in 1908, and at the Salon des Artistes Français in 1921. Not included in the first Salons of the Société de la Gravure Originale en Couleurs, he appeared there only in 1920 with *The Chair Caner* (edition of twenty, 100 francs) and *Old Man Walking* (edition of twenty, 80 francs). M. G.

23 *Old Man Walking*
Vieux Marcheur, 1906 (IFF 5)
*Aquatint, 52.7 x 35 cm
Signed: lr monogram M.N.
Bibliothèque Nationale, D. 3302 (2 April 1931, Musée du Luxembourg); Dc 439, t. I.

24 *Chaff*
L'Ivraie, 1906 (IFF 8)
Etching and aquatint, 55 x 31.2 cm
Signed: lr monogram M.N.
Bibliothèque Nationale, Dc 439, t. I.

25 *The Chair Caner*
Le Rempailleur, 1906 (IFF 10)
*Etching and aquatint, 49.8 x 36.4 cm
Signed: ll "Le Rempailleur 9/20," lr "Georges Bruyer," monogram M.N.
Bibliothèque Nationale, D. 3302 (2 April 1931, Musée du Luxembourg); Dc 439, t. I.

26 *The Duenna*
La Duègne, c. 1906 (IFF 12)
*Aquatint touched with pigment, 44.5 x 33.8 cm
Signed: lr in pencil "Georges Bruyer," ll "11/20"
Zimmerli Art Museum, David A. and Mildred H. Morse Art Acquisition Fund.

Félix BUHOT (1847-1898)

Buhot was a prolific printmaker specializing in all aspects of the intaglio process. Very active from the mid-1870s through the early 1890s, he was attracted to Japanese motifs and aesthetics, and especially to Japanese papers and inks. These interests are best seen in his 1883 album *Japonisme, Ten Etchings* for which his friend Henri Guérard created the cover design. Essentially a black-and-white printmaker, his 1878 experiments in color etching *à la poupée* were symptomatic of his exploration and exploitation of the atmospheric effects of etching. P. D. C.
[Gustave Bourcard, *Félix Buhot: catalogue descriptif de son œuvre gravé* (1899 and revised edition by James Goodfriends, New York: Martin Gordon Inc., 1979)]

27 *The National Holiday of 30th June on boulevard Clichy*
La Fête nationale du 30 juin au boulevard Clichy, 1878 (B 127—IV; IFF 91)
*Etching and aquatint, gilded margins, 31.5 x 23.8 cm
Signed: ll in image "Félix Buhot/1er juillet 1878

boulevard Clichy" ll in margin "F. Buhot pinxt sc.," lc "La Fête nationale du 30 juin/au boulevard Clichy," lr "L'univers"
Bibliothèque Nationale, D. 1979—00247 (14 March 1979, Mrs. Bacquier and Gedigier, M. Reiner); Ef 415d, t. III.

28 *The Small Funeral*
Le Petit Enterrement, 1883 (B 154)
Etching, aquatint, and roulette, printed in blue, 8.5 x 11.4 cm
Signed: ul in plate artist's monogram in reverse
Zimmerli Art Museum, Friends Purchase Fund.

Mary CASSATT (1844-1926)

Born in Pittsburgh, U.S.A., Mary Cassatt was a pupil of John Sartain at the Philadelphia School of Fine Art (1860-64) and then spent time with the etcher Carlo Raimondi at the Academy of Parma (1871-72). She moved to Paris in 1874 and became involved with Degas and the Impressionists, exhibiting her work with them from 1877 to 1881. Under the influence of Degas, Mary Cassatt began to work in etching, drypoint, aquatint, and softground. In 1890 she visited the exhibition of Japanese color woodblock prints organized by Siegfried Bing. Her first attempts in printing in color date from this year. In April 1891 Durand-Ruel exhibited ten etchings (aquatint and drypoint) printed in color with the aid of Leroy. In November-December 1893 these ten etchings and also *The Kitchen Garden* and *The Banjo Lesson* were shown again at Durand-Ruel. From 1890 to 1897 she executed twenty-two works in etching, softground, and aquatint, and one color monotype; between 1900 and 1910 she made four color drypoints. In 1923, at her request, Eugène Delâtre reprinted them and certain plates were reworked. M. G.
[Adelyn D. Breeskin, *The Graphic Work of Mary Cassatt, A Catalogue Raisonné* (New York: H. Bittner and Co., 1948)]
[Nancy Mowll Mathews and Barbara Stern Shapiro, *Mary Cassatt: The Color Prints* (New York: Abrams, 1989)]

29 *The Tub*
Bain d'enfant, 1890-91 (B 143—XI; MS 5—XVII)
Drypoint, softground, and aquatint, 31.6 x 24.7 cm
Signed: lc in pencil "Édition de 25 épreuves," lr in pencil "imprimée par l'artiste et M. Leroy/Mary Cassatt," lc artist's monogram
Bibliothèque Nationale, D. 14151 (5 July 1963, Musée d'Art Moderne); Ce 4 rés., t. II.

30 *The Lamp*
La Lampe, 1890-91 (B 144—III; MS 6—IV)
Drypoint, softground, and aquatint, 32.3 x 25.3 cm
Signed: lr in pencil "Édition de 25 épreuves imprimées par l'artiste et M. Leroy/Mary Cassatt," lc artist's monogram
Bibliothèque Nationale, D. 14151; Ce 4 rés., t. II.

31 *In the Omnibus*
Intérieur d'un Tramway passant un pont, 1890-91 (145—IV; MS 7—VII)
Drypoint and aquatint in pink, 36.4 x 26.6 cm
Signed: lr in pencil "à Monsieur Leroy/Mary Cassatt," lc artist's monogram
Bibliothèque Nationale, A. 8804 (22 June 1921, M. Strölin); Ce 4 rés., t. II.

32 *The Letter*
La Lettre, 1890-91 (B 146—III; MS 8—IV)
Drypoint and aquatint, 34.6 x 22.8 cm
Signed: lr in pencil "Édition de 25 épreuves imprimées par l'artiste et M. Leroy/Mary Cassatt," lc artist's monogram
Bibliothèque Nationale D. 14151; Ce 4 Rés., t. II.

33 *The Fitting*
Jeune Femme essayant une robe, 1890-91 (B 147—V; MS 9—VI)
Drypoint and aquatint, 37.8 x 25.6 cm
Signed: lc artist's monogram
Bibliothèque Nationale, A. 09272 (11 February 1936, M. Guiot); Ce 4 rés., t. II.

34 *The Toilette*
La Toilette, 1890-91 (B 148—V; MS 10—IV)
Drypoint and aquatint, 36.4 x 26.6 cm
Signed: lr in pencil "Édition de 25 épreuves imprimées par l'artiste et M. Leroy/Mary Cassatt," lc artist's monogram
Bibliothèque Nationale, D. 14151; Ce 4 rés., t. II.

35 *Mother's Kiss*
Le Baiser maternel, 1890-91 (B 149—IV; MS 11—V)
Drypoint and aquatint, 34.8 x 22.9 cm
Signed: lr in pencil "Imprimée par l'artiste et M. Leroy/Mary Cassatt/25 épreuves"
Bibliothèque Nationale A. 09272; Ce 4 rés., t. II.

36 *Maternal Caress*
Enfant nue, 1890-91 (B 150—III; MS 12—VI)
Drypoint, softground, and aquatint, 36.7 x 26.9 cm
Signed: lc in pencil "Édition de 25 épreuves imprimées par l'artiste et M. Leroy/Mary Cassatt," lc artist's monogram
Bibliothèque Nationale, D. 14151; Ce 4 rés., t. II.

37 *Afternoon Tea Party*
Le Thé, 1890-91 (B 151—III; MS 13—V)
Drypoint and aquatint touched with gold, 34.5 x 26.9 cm
Signed: lc in pencil "Édition de 25 épreuves imprimées par l'artiste et M. Leroy/Mary Cassatt," lc artist's monogram
Bibliothèque Nationale, D. 14151; Ce 4 rés., t. II.

38 *The Coiffure*
Femme se coiffant, 1891 (B 152—IV; MS 14—V)
Drypoint and aquatint, 36.6 x 26.7 cm
Signed: lc in pencil "Édition de 25 épreuves imprimées par l'artiste et M. Leroy/Mary Cassatt," lc artist's monogram
Bibliothèque Nationale, D. 14151; Ce 4 rés., t. II.

39 *The Banjo Lesson*
La Leçon de banjo, c. 1893 (B 156—IV; MS 16—IV)
Drypoint and aquatint, 29.8 x 23.6 cm
Signed: lr in pencil "Mary Cassatt"
Bibliothèque Nationale, from Laffon collection sold in Zurich on 7-8 April 1938; A. 09458 (29 April 1938); Ce 4 rés., t. II.

40 *By the Pond*
Jeune Mère dans un parc devant un bassin, c. 1896 (B 161—IV; MS 21—IV)
Etching, drypoint, and aquatint, 32.9 x 42.9 cm
Signed: lr in pencil "Mary Cassatt"
Bibliothèque Nationale, A. 10442 (auction, Paris, 12 December 1947); Ce 4 rés., t. II.

41 *Under the Horse Chestnut*
Sur l'herbe, 1898 (B 162—III; MS 20—III)
Drypoint and aquatint, 40.7 x 28.8 cm
Signed: lr in pencil "Mary Cassatt," ll in pencil "Offert à la Bibliothèque nationale/par la Société de l'estampe nouvelle/ Eug. Rodrigues Pdt"
Bibliothèque Nationale, D. 9476 (M. Rodrigues, 12 February 1900); Ce 4 rés., t. II.

Edgar CHAHINE (1874-1947)
Born in Venice of Armenian parents, Chahine moved to Paris in 1895 and studied at the Académie Julian. He created his first etchings in 1897, and Edmond Sagot soon became his dealer and publisher. Under the instruction of Eugène Delâtre, Chahine developed a two-plate system of color printing, the first plate carrying the basic outline and tonal qualities of the composition and the second, in aquatint or softground, colored à la poupée. Chahine created over four hundred monochrome or color etchings throughout his life. His most important work in color etching, however, was during the first decade of the twentieth century, when he explored the popular themes of elegant Parisians, prostitutes, circus performers and, in the tradition of Raffaëlli, the impoverished and homeless.
P. D. C.
[R. Tabanelli, *Edgar Chahine, catalogue de l'œuvre gravé* (Milan: Il Mercante di Stampe, 1977)]

42 *The Terrace*
La Terrasse, 1899 (T 26—IV)
Drypoint and aquatint, 35 x 29.9 cm
Signed: ll in plate "Edgar Chahine," ll in pencil "Edgar Chahine," lr in pencil "La Terrasse"
Bibliothèque Nationale, D. 724 (E. Chahine, 15 February 1908); Dc 373a, t. I.

43 *Un Couple de Soupeuses*, 1901 (T 68—V)
Drypoint and aquatint, 38.9 x 19.5 cm
Signed: ll in pencil "Edgar Chahine"
Bibliothèque Nationale, A. 1984—73520 (sale, 14 November 1984); Dc 373a, t. I.

44 *The Wrestlers: A Hold*
Les Lutteurs, une prise, 1902 (T 84—IV)
Drypoint, softground, and aquatint, 30.4 x 49.5 cm
Signed: ll in pencil "Edgar Chahine," lr in pencil "Une prise"
Bibliothèque Nationale, D. 724; Dc 373a, t. I.

45 *The Tightrope Walker*
La Danseuse de corde, 1906 (T 162—II)
*Etching and softground, 49.6 x 33.9 cm
Signed: ll in plate "E. Chahine," ll in pencil "Edgar Chahine 13/40"
Zimmerli Art Museum, David A. and Mildred H. Morse Art Acquisition Fund.

46 *The Streetwalkers*
Les Trotteuses, 1907 (T 234—II)
*Etching, aquatint, and softground, 46.4 x 33.1 cm
Signed: ll in pencil "Edgar Chahine," lr in pencil "Les Trotteuses"
Bibliothèque Nationale, D. 724; Dc 373a, t. II.

Charles COTTET (1863-1925)
Having studied at the Académie Julian and then under Puvis de Chavannes, Charles Cot-

tet discovered Brittany in 1885; this region remained his principal inspiration. Around 1892 he became involved with the Nabis—Bonnard, Vuillard, and Roussel—and, from 1895 began to experiment with lithography. In 1905 he produced some etched "studies of emphasis and colour": *The Sisters of Saint-Esprit around a Coffin* bears witness, through the interplay of flat planes of color, to the continuing Nabi influence. At the second Salon of the Société de la Gravure Originale en Couleurs that same year, he presented eleven color etchings, including *Fishing Boats at Night* and *Fishing Boats at Sunset* (editions of 150, 80 and 50 francs), *Fishermen Fleeing the Storm*, and *Little Dancer* (editions of 100, 50 francs). In 1907 he exhibited three prints under the title *In the Land of the Sea* (edition of 100, 100 francs) and, in 1909, a triptych of the same name, produced with Ch. Coppier (edition of 160, 600 francs). Cottet's *Fishermen Fleeing the Storm*, *Fishing Boats at Night*, and *Fishing Boats* appeared in Georges Petit's 1906 catalogue and, in 1911, Cottet exhibited fifty-nine etchings at his gallery, including some prints with variations of color from the same plate. He also exhibited at the Salons of the Société Nationale des Beaux Arts and of the Société des Peintres-Graveurs Français. His themes continued to evoke Brittany—landscapes featuring the Crozon peninsula, Penmarc'h Point and scenes from the lives of fishermen—but he also found inspiration in the feminine form, and in particular the famous Loïe Fuller. He was made Chevalier de la Légion d'Honneur in 1900 at the end of the Universal Exhibition where he received a gold medal, and became Officier in 1912. Once he had been officially recognized, the State regularly bought his prints for the Musée du Luxembourg; these were later given to the Print Department of the Bibliothèque Nationale.
M. G.

47a *Dancer*
Danseuse, c. 1904 (IFF 2—I)
Etching in ochre-red, 11.8 x 18 cm
Signed: lr monogram M.N.
Bibliothèque Nationale, D. 3302 (2 April 1931, Musée du Luxembourg); Dc 440.

47b *Dancer*
Danseuse, c. 1904 (IFF 2—IV)
Etching in black and red, 11.3 x 18.5 cm
Signed: lr monogram M.N.
Bibliothèque Nationale, D. 3302; Dc 440.

47c *Dancer*
Danseuse, c. 1904 (IFF 2—III)
Etching in red and purple, 11.6 x 18 cm
Signed: lr monogram M.N.
Bibliothèque Nationale, D. 3302; Dc 440.

47d *Dancer*
Danseuse, c. 1904 (IFF 2—II)
Etching, aquatint and roulette in red and black, 11.4 x 18.4 cm
Signed: lr monogram M.N.
Bibliothèque Nationale, D. 3302; Dc 440.

48 *Fishermen Fleeing the Storm*
Pêcheurs fuyant devant l'orage, c. 1905 (IFF 2)

Etching, aquatint and roulette printed in blue, 49.4 x 39.7 cm
Signed: ll in pencil "No. 14," monogram M.N.
Bibliothèque Nationale, D. 3302; Dc 440.

49 Boats in the Harbour at Sunset
Barques dans le port au soleil couchant, 1905 (IFF 2)
Etching, drypoint, and aquatint, 24 x 31 cm
Signed: lr in pencil "Ch. Cottet," lr monogram M.N., r in margin monogram "Atelier Charles Cottet"
Bibliothèque Nationale, D. 3302; Dc 440.

50a Boats
Bateaux, c. 1905 (IFF 2)
*Etching and aquatint in black, red, and yellow, 12.9 x 17.9 cm
Signed: ll in plate "Ch. Cottet," ll in pencil "No. 6," lr in pencil "Ch. Cottet," lr monogram M.N.
Bibliothèque Nationale, D. 3302; Dc 440.

50b Boats
Bateaux, c. 1905 (IFF 2)
Etching and aquatint in pale brown, 12.8 x 18 cm
Signed: ll in plate "Ch. Cottet," lr monogram M.N.
Bibliothèque Nationale, D. 3302; Dc 440.

51 Sisters of Saint-Esprit around a Coffin
Sœurs du Saint-Esprit autour d'un cercueil, 1906 (IFF 2)
Drypoint and aquatint, 32.7 x 42 cm
Signed: lr in pencil "Ch. Cottet," ll in pencil "No. 18," lr monogram M.N.
Bibliothèque Nationale, D. 3302.

52 Women Sitting, Ouessant
Femmes assises, Ouessant, 1906 (IFF 2)
Etching and aquatint, 31 x 41.5 cm
Signed: lr monogram M.N.
Bibliothèque Nationale, D. 3302; Dc 440.

Auguste-Marie DELÂTRE (1822-1907)
Trained by painter-etcher Charles Jacque and by Louis Marvy, Auguste Delâtre founded his printing business in 1844. On July 8, 1852 he obtained a printer's licence for Paris; he exchanged this for a licence specifically for Montmartre on September 5, 1857, but then replaced it with a Parisian one on December 19, 1857. Intending to make his workshop into the leading printing atelier in Paris, Auguste Delâtre tried to perfect his printing techniques by varying the application of ink. Based on the Left Bank, he became the official printer for the Société des Aquafortistes in 1863. In 1860 he was called to London to set up an etching department; when the Commune destroyed his Parisian workshops, he returned to London and printed works by Whistler between 1871 and 1876. On his return to Paris he set up in Montmartre at 2 rue Tourlaque and then 87 rue Lepic. He printed for the Impressionists, for Charles Meryon and for Félicien Rops, but tended to print with too much verve, to such an extent that Desboutin called it "etching with a cataplasm." In 1887 Delâtre wrote a treatise entitled Eau-forte, pointe-sèche et vernis mou (with the aid of Rops for the last part). For him etching was a secondary experience; a testing ground that might enable him to refine his application of ink. He produced some drypoint monotypes that are comparable to mobile etching by Count Lepic and monotypes

by Adolphe Appian. The three vignettes of Effects of the Moon (c. 1880), like Night (1883), were first defined by a light working of drypoint and roulette; Delâtre then covered the surface of the plate with an abrasive; with the aid of a rag he wiped the surface with somber colors, brown or bronze-green, leaving on the copper plate varied tones of ink, like a veil, to achieve the glaucous quality of moonlight. The sober but luminous impressions are proof, as Michel Melot states, that Delâtre was "not only the principal printer for the Impressionists, but above all an Impressionist printer." M. G.

53 Landscape
Paysage, c. 1880 (IFF 8)
*Drypoint and roulette monotype, 9.3 x 13.3 cm
Signed: lr in plate "A. Delâtre del et sc"
Bibliothèque Nationale, A. 9704; Ef 542.

54 Night
La Nuit, 1883 (IFF 8)
*Drypoint monotype, 15.8 x 11.8 cm
Signed: lr in plate "Aug Delâtre 1883"
Bibliothèque Nationale, A. 9704 (Mme. M. Le Garrec, 24 October 1942); Ef 542.

Eugène DELÂTRE (1854-1938)
Trained by his father Auguste Delâtre, Eugène Delâtre was not content simply to work with him and take over the direction of the printshop on rue Lepic in 1907. He put his experience to the service of most of the etchers of his time and played a fundamental role in the establishment of color etching. He attempted to find the equivalent of the inking processes used in Japanese woodblocks for copper plates. Around 1895 he substituted the principle of etching au repérage (one plate per color) for inking à la poupée: filling the etched lines and grains with a bistre tone, adding the colors with a pad or poupée, and then printing the plate. In his treatise on aquatint, Pierre Gatier wrote that Delâtre's printing à la poupée was achieving considerable success and the renaissance of color etching was beginning. The Musée de Saint-Denis has a good collection of color prints donated in 1978 by Mme Delâtre, and their dedications bear witness to the place occupied by Eugène Delâtre in the world of color etching: etchings were given to him by Boutet de Monvel, Houdard, Latenay, Luigini, Ranft, Robbe, Roux-Champion, and Müller. Nonetheless he was criticized for his surface tone and for his blending of colors, to the detriment of pure tones, which made prints monotonous and uniform. As a printer, however, he was capable of printing au repérage and following artist's instructions, as is demonstrated by the permission to print signed by Rassenfosse for his Woman Sitting with Red Shawl and Green Hat. Eugène Delâtre began to etch with acid and drypoint in 1876, and first attended the Salon des Artistes Français in 1881-82 with watercolors and drawings of Montmartre. His color etchings were exhibited at the Salon of the Société Nationale des Beaux Arts: in 1893, In a Garden; in 1894, Portrait of Auguste Delâtre and The Dressmaker; in 1895, five prints, including Grandfather and

Child and Marcel. In February 1898 an exhibition at the Durand-Ruel gallery featured work by Francis Jourdain and Delâtre, including landscapes, scenes of children, and Paris Casino; the exhibition was only a limited success and L'Estampe et l'Affiche gave it a grudging review. In May 1900 Delâtre donated the color etching Village Street at Night (inked à la poupée, edition of forty-five, seven states) to L'Estampe Nouvelle. From 1904 he participated in the Salons of the Société de la Gravure Originale en Couleurs; he was also printer for the society. Except in 1908, 1911 and 1913, he presented genre scenes and landscapes in editions of 100 to 200 at a price of 35 to 100 francs, which is much more than the "two, three, four, five francs . . ." indicated by Pissarro, who in 1896 had claimed that low prices were the main reason for Delâtre's success . . . and for his own failure. Finally Eugène Delâtre came back to black and white, as in the art of Jacques Beurdeley and Adolphe Beaufrère. M. G.

55a Village of Bevillers (North)
Village de Bevillers (Nord), c. 1891-92 (I)
Etching and aquatint, 14 x 22.9 cm
Signed: lr in blue crayon "Eug. Delâtre/No. 19," lc artist's monogram in red ink, Lugt 742
Bibliothèque Nationale, A. 1985—73675 (30 April 1985); Ef 463, t. I.

55b Village of Bevillers (North)
Village de Bevillers (Nord), c. 1891 (II)
Etching, softground, and aquatint, 14 x 22.8 cm
Signed: lr in blue crayon "Eug. Delâtre"
Bibliothèque Nationale, A. 1985—73675; Ef 463, t. I.

56 On the Boulevards
Sur les boulevards, 1893 (IFF 4)
Drypoint and aquatint, 25.5 x 11.5 cm
Signed: ll in plate "Eug. Delâtre/1893," lr in blue crayon "Eug. Delâtre/No. 18," lc artist's monogram in red ink, Lugt 742, lr monogram M. N.
Bibliothèque Nationale, D. 3302 (Musée du Luxembourg, 2 April 1931); Ef 463, t. I.

57 In a Garden
Dans un jardin, 1893
Etching and aquatint, 25.3 x 18.7 cm
Signed: ll in plate "Eug. Delâtre 1893," lr in pencil "no. 80/Eug. Delâtre," ll in pencil (different hand) "Première gravure en couleurs/exposée par Eug. Delâtre au Salon de 1893/C. Quesneville," lc in pencil "Dans un jardin pl. détruite/tir. à 51 épreuves," lc artist's monogram in red ink, Lugt 742
Bibliothèque Nationale, D. 8206 (30 January 1952, M. Quesneville); Ef 463, t. I.

58a Bust of Parisian Woman
Tête de la Parisienne, 1893 (IFF3—I)
Etching and aquatint, 18.2 x 13.4 cm
Signed: lr in blue crayon "Eug. Delâtre," lr on paper "Ép d'état," artist's monogram in ochre ink, Lugt 742
Bibliothèque Nationale, A. 9890 (Collection of Jules Lieure, 24 December 1943); Ef 463, t. I.

58b Bust of Parisian Woman
Tête de la Parisienne, 1893 (IFF 3—II)
Etching, drypoint, and aquatint, 18.2 x 13.3 cm

Signed: lr in plate "Eug. Delâtre 1893," lc in blue crayon "Eug. Delâtre," artist's monogram in ochre ink, Lugt 742
Bibliothèque Nationale, A. 9890; Ef 463, t. I.

59 *Portrait of Huysmans*
Portrait de Huysmans, 1893 (IFF 12)
Etching and aquatint, 32.2 x 23.9 cm
Signed: lr in plate in reverse "Eug. Delâtre," lr in blue crayon "Eug. Delâtre no. 39," ll on border blind stamp of L'*Estampe Originale*
Zimmerli Art Museum.

60 *Self-Portrait*
Autoportrait, c. 1894 (IFF 5)
Etching, roulette, and aquatint, 29 x 23.2 cm
Signed: ll in pencil "9/30," lr in pencil "Eug. Delâtre," lc artist's monogram
Bibliothèque Nationale, D. 1994; Ef 463, t. I.

61 *In Brittany, Etchings and Lithographs by Maufra*
En Bretagne. Eaux-fortes et lithographies par Maufra, 1894
Aquatint and etching, 45.7 x 31.8 cm
Signed: lr in plate "Eug. Delâtre 94," lr monograms of Eugène and Auguste Delâtre
(Cover for album published by L'*Estampe Originale*)
Zimmerli Art Museum, David A. and Mildred H. Morse Art Acquisition Fund.

62 *Portrait of Auguste Delâtre*
Portrait d'Auguste Delâtre, 1894 (IFF5)
Etching and aquatint, 29 x 23.2 cm
Signed: ll in plate "Eug. Delâtre 94," lr in blue crayon "no. 76/ Eug. Delâtre/à M. Eug. Béjot/ bien amicalement," lc artist's monogram in orange ink, Lugt 742
Bibliothèque Nationale, D. 3570 (legs Eugène Béjot, 9 March 1933); Ef 463, t. I.

63 *The Dressmaker*
La Couturière, c. 1894 (IFF 5—VII)
Etching, drypoint, roulette, and aquatint, 53.5 x 26.6 cm
Signed: lc in plate "Eug. Delâtre," lr in ink "7ème état 2ème ép./ Eug. Delâtre," lc artist's monogram, Lugt 742
Bibliothèque Nationale, A. 9725 (Henri Petiet, 19 November 1942); Ef 463, t. I.

64a *Woman with a Parasol*
Femme à l'ombrelle, c. 1895 (IFF 6)
Etching, drypoint, and aquatint in yellow, pink, blue, brown, and black, 32.1 x 24.3 cm
Signed: ll in pencil "53/75," lr in pencil "Eug. Delâtre"
Bibliothèque Nationale, D. 2001 (A. Delâtre, 20 October 1921); Ef 463, t. I.

64b *Woman with a Parasol*
Femme à l'ombrelle, c. 1895 (IFF 6)
Etching, drypoint, and aquatint in blue, pink, green, and black, 32.2 x 24.3 cm
Signed: lr in blue crayon "no. 58/ Eug. Delâtre," lr title in pencil, lr monogram M.N.
Bibliothèque Nationale, D. 3302 (Musée du Luxembourg, 2 April 1931); Ef 463, t. I.

65 *Marcel*, 1895
Etching and aquatint, 17.4 x 24.8 cm
Signed: lr in blue crayon "No. 5 Eug. Delâtre," lr in plate "E. Delâtre 95," lr in plate artist's monogram,

lc in pencil "Marcel, tir. à 28 ép."
Zimmerli Art Museum, David A. and Mildred H. Morse Art Acquisition Fund.

66 *Grandfather and Child*
Le Grand-Père et l'enfant, 1895
Etching, drypoint, and aquatint, 39.7 x 25 cm
Signed: lr in blue crayon "no. 10/ Eug. Delâtre," lr monogram M.N., lc artist's monogram, Lugt 742, lr title in pencil
Bibliothèque Nationale, D. 3302; Ef 463, t. I.

67 *The Plot*
Le Complot, c. 1895 (IFF 6)
Etching, drypoint, and aquatint, 29.3 x 17.8 cm
Signed: lr in blue crayon " Eug. Delâtre no. 22," ll title in pencil, lc artist's monogram in red ink, Lugt 742
Bibliothèque Nationale, D. 2001 (A. Delâtre, 20 October 1921); Ef 463, t. I.

68 *At the Café-Concert*
Au café-concert, c. 1895
Etching and aquatint, 19.2 x 13.2 cm
Signed: lr in blue crayon "Eug. Delâtre," lc monogram "A.D." (Auguste Delâtre)
Zimmerli Art Museum, David A. and Mildred H. Morse Art Acquisition Fund.

69 *Portrait of E. Gressin*
Portrait d'E. Gressin, 1896 (IFF6)
*Drypoint and softground, 30 x 16 cm
Signed: ll in plate "à l'ami E. Gressin/ le bon poète," lr in plate "Eug. Delâtre, 1896," lr in blue crayon "Eug. Delâtre," monogram M. N.
Bibliothèque Nationale, D. 3302; Ef 463, t. I.

70 *Death Wearing Furs*
La Mort vêtue de fourrures, c. 1897
Etching and aquatint, 51 x 33 cm
Signed: lr in pencil "Eug. Delâtre," "amicalement à M. Rodrigues," "no. 12"
Zimmerli Art Museum, Herbert Littman Purchase Fund.

71 *Man Lying in the Grass*
Homme couché dans l'herbe, c. 1898 (IFF 8)
Etching, roulette, and aquatint, 7.1 x 11.5 cm
Signed: lr in plate "E.D.," lr below image in pencil "Eug. Delâtre," lr monogram M.N.
Bibliothèque Nationale, D. 3302; Ef 463, t. I.

72 *Child in the Park*
Enfant au Square, c. 1900
Etching and aquatint, 23 x 15.7 cm
Signed: ll in plate "Eug. Delâtre"
Zimmerli Art Museum, Class of 1932 Art Purchase Fund.

73 *Singing Lesson*
Leçon de chant, c. 1901
Etching, drypoint, and aquatint, 29.6 x 21 cm
Signed: lr in blue crayon "Eug. Delâtre" and below in pencil "no. 16/25," lc in pencil "Leçon de chant"
Bibliothèque Nationale, D. 2001; Ef 463, t. I.

74 *The Seine at Genevilliers*
La Seine à Genevilliers, c. 1903 (IFF 15)
Softground and aquatint, 32.8 x 49.8 cm
Signed: ll in pencil "31/50," lr "Eug. Delâtre," lr "La Seine à Genevilliers"
Bibliothèque Nationale, D. 2001; Ef 463, t. I.

75 *Eaux-Fortes originales. Exposition*, c. 1898
*Etching and aquatint, 9.5 x 12.8 cm
Signed: ll in plate "Eug. Delâtre"
Zimmerli Art Museum.

Henry-Julien DETOUCHE (1854-1913)
Detouche's earliest known etching in color is *At the Theater* of 1886; in 1891 he became a member of the Société des Peintres-Graveurs along with Boutet, Bracquemond, Buhot, Guérard, Lepère, and Rivière. His travels to Spain in the mid-1890s inspired Spanish subject matter in his work and resulted in the publication of the book *De Montmartre à Montserrat* in 1899. A longtime resident of Montmartre, Detouche probably worked at the studio of Eugène Delâtre and was acquainted with fellow cat-lover, Steinlen. In 1905 Detouche participated in the exhibition of the Société de la Gravure Originale en Couleurs held at the Georges Petit gallery. P. D. C.

76 *At the Theater*
Au Théâtre, 1886
*Etching, 36.5 x 27.5 cm
Signed: ll in pencil "Henry Detouche," ll in plate "Henry Detouche 1886"
Zimmerli Art Museum, David A. and Mildred H. Morse Art Acquisition Fund.

77 *To the Glory of the Cat*
A la gloire du chat, c. 1904 (IFF 29)
*Etching and aquatint, 40.2 x 30 cm
Signed: ll in plate "Henry Detouche," ll "épreuve d'essai," c "A la gloire du chat"
Bibliothèque Nationale, A. 7922 (L. Delteil, 14 June 1913); Ef 442.

78 *La Clavelito in El Garrotin*
La Clavelito dans El Garrotin, c. 1910 (IFF 17)
Etching and aquatint, 22.8 x 16.9 cm
Signed: ll in plate " H. Detouche," lc in pencil "Henry Detouche—La Clavelito dans El Garrotin—5—60"
Bibliothèque Nationale, Ef 442.

Émile-Alfred DEZAUNAY (1854-1938)
Born in Nantes, Émile Dezaunay was a pupil of Puvis de Chavannes and Élie Delaunay at the École de Beaux-Arts in Paris. In 1890 he stayed at Marie-Jeanne Gloanec's inn at Pont-Aven with his friend Maxime Maufra and met Gauguin, Sérusier, Meyer de Haan and Charles Filiger. Like Maufra, whose studio on Place Ravignon he frequented, Dezaunay concentrated on etching and color aquatint. An exhibition of his work was held by Moline in rue Laffitte from February 15 to March 14 1897, and Maufra created the poster, *The Way to St-Jean-du-Doigt*, for the exhibition. On March 25, 1898, Dezaunay put a collection of his work to auction at the Hôtel Drouot; Arsène Alexandre wrote the preface to the catalogue. Dezaunay exhibited at the Universal Exposition in 1900 and at the Bernheim gallery in 1902. A founding member of the Salon d'Automne, he also took part many times in the Salons of the Tuileries, the Artistes Français, and the Artistes Indépendants. In Nantes he was involved with the Société des Artistes Nantais (which in 1902 became the

Société des Artistes Bretons) and with the Amis des Arts. His work—scenes of Parisian and Breton life—was sold by Sagot, rue de Chateaudun. M. G.

---

79 *Mass in Brittany*
La Messe en Bretagne, c. 1900
Etching and aquatint, 32 x 42 cm
Signed: lr in pencil "Dezaunay," lr Sagot blind stamp, ll in pencil "12/50"
Zimmerli Art Museum, David A. and Mildred H. Morse Art Acquisition Fund.

80 *Plougastel Daoulas,* c. 1900
*Aquatint touched with watercolor, 25 x 32 cm
Signed: lr in pencil "Dezaunay," "Plougastel Daoulas"
Zimmerli Art Museum, Marion and Allan Maitlin Purchase Fund.

81 *Little Beggar, Pleyben*
Petite Mendiante de Pleyben, c. 1900
Etching and aquatint, 41.8 x 32 cm
Signed: lr in pencil "Dezaunay," ll in pencil "15/50"
Zimmerli Art Museum, David A. and Mildred H. Morse Art Acquisition Fund.

Pierre GATIER (1878-1944)
A pupil of Blanc, Cormon, Thirion, and Le Couteux, Pierre Gatier launched into etching in 1900 with drypoint, etching and aquatint in color: *The Milliner* dates from this year, although it was only exhibited in 1908 at the fifth Salon of the Société de la Gravure Originale en Couleurs. This was the first time that Gatier participated in the Salon; he showed eight works, their editions ranging from forty to one hundred. He returned in 1909 with eight works, including *The Ice Palace,* and also contributed in the years 1910 to 1913. In 1909 he became one of the artists published by Georges Petit; in 1911 Petit was in possession of the plates for *La Journée des Poules, Champs-Élysées, At the Derby, The Parisian Seasons, Rue de la Paix,* and *Pack of Hounds, Chantilly,* all of which were printed in editions of 120 to 150. Thereafter his work was published by Edmond Sagot and then Marcel Guiot until 1931. His elegant prints are representative of the worldly tastes of Paris during the Belle Époque. His research in color etching was interrupted by World War I, as can be seen in his *Traité de l'aquatinte en trois couleurs,* written beween 1910 and 1920 but never published. He only took up color etching again in 1928-29 for the Société de l'Estampe Contemporaine. M. G.

82 *The Milliner*
La Modiste, c. 1900 (IFF 2)
Etching and aquatint, 31.5 x 20 cm
Signed: lr in plate "P. Gatier," ll in pencil "10/50 la modiste," lr in pencil "P. Gatier," blind stamp "Ed. Sagot Éditeur"
Bibliothèque Nationale, A. 11158 (31 May 1954); AA3 Gatier.

Marie GAUTIER (1870-?)
Little is known of this artist who, like Guérard, Cassatt, Rivière, and Houdard, was interested in Japanese aesthetics and color etching. Gautier exhibited her color etchings as early as 1893 at the Salon of the Société

Nationale des Beaux-Arts and throughout the next fifteen years at such public displays as the exhibition of the Société des Peintres-Graveurs Français (1897), the Salon d'Automne (1905), and the Salon of the Société Nationale des Beaux-Arts (1907). P. D. C.

83 *Mouse*
Souris, c. 1893
*Etching and aquatint, 8.9 x 45.3 cm
Signed: ll in pencil "Marie Gautier," lr in pencil "10 épreuves no. 5"
Zimmerli Art Museum, David A. and Mildred H. Morse Art Acquisition Fund.

84 *Saint-Briac,* c. 1893
Etching, aquatint, and softground touched with watercolor, 25.7 x 35.7 cm
Signed: ll on image two versions of artist's monogram, ll in pencil "Marie Gautier 1/10"
Zimmerli Art Museum, Carleton A. Holstrom Art Purchase Fund.

Henri-Charles GUÉRARD (1846-97)
A friend and associate of Édouard Manet, Guérard married the latter's student and model Eva Gonzales in 1879. Guérard was one of the most prolific printmakers of the nineteenth century (the Bibliothèque Nationale has 705 prints by him). He experimented in all media and succumbed early in his career to the attractions of Japanese prints. He produced reproductions of Japanese arts and crafts copied after works in private collections (such as that of the art critic Philippe Burty) for the *Gazette des Beaux-Arts* (1875) and for Louis Gonse's important history *L'Art Japonais* (1883). Influenced by the Japanese use of color, Guérard, by the early 1880s, regularly incorporated color in his work by means of one-color printing or the *à la poupée* technique; it was however around 1885 that Guérard, as his own printer, thoroughly mastered the multiplate system of printing based upon the eighteenth-century method of three primary colors plus black. His examples of color printing *au repérage* published in *Le Livre moderne* and presented at the first exhibition of the Société des Peintres-Graveurs introduced his contemporaries to the process just as the question of color printmaking was emerging as a controversial topic within academic circles and as a new possibility for artistic expression among the avant-garde. P. D. C.
[Claudie Bertin, *Henri Guérard (1846-1897) l'œuvre gravé,* 3 vols, mémoire de l'école du Louvre (1975)]
[G. Bourcard, Félix Buhot, *Catalogue descriptif de son œuvre gravé* (1899 and revised edition by James Goodfriends, New York: Martin Gordon Inc., 1979)]

85 *Japonisme. Ten Etchings*
Japonisme. Dix Eaux Fortes, 1883 (IFF 10; CB 418; BG 11—II)
Etching and aquatint in red, 26.2 x 17.9 cm
Signed: ul "JAPONISME, DIX EAUX-FORTES," c in plate "Par/Félix Buhot/avril 1883"
(Cover for Félix Buhot's album)
Bibliothèque Nationale, Ef 415d, t. I.

86a *In the Garden*
Au jardin, before 1886 (CB 109, final state)
Aquatint, drypoint, and roulette, 41 x 34.5 cm
Signed: in plate "H. Guérard pinxit et sculpcit"
Bibliothèque Nationale, Ef 477, t. III.

86b *In the Garden*
Au jardin, before 1886 (CB 109)
Series of etchings printed in color from three plates. This exhibition includes six states of the print in blue, two states in red and three states in yellow, then a series of six proofs each combining two tones, and finally three proofs with the three tones.
Bibliothèque Nationale, Ef 477, t. III.

87 *Punchinello*
Le Polichinelle, 1885-87 (CB 116)
Etching, 15.9 x 7.7 cm
Zimmerli Art Museum.

88 *Ten Business Cards Belonging to the Artist*
Dix Cartes de visite de l'auteur, before 1888 (CB 370)
Etching, softground, and aquatint in red on mauve paper, 37.3 x 24.1 cm
Signed: lr in pencil "H. Guérard," lc artist's monogram
Bibliothèque Nationale, D. 99996 (J. Gruyer, 23 July 1975); Ef 477, t. X.

89a *Twenty Grotesque Masks*
Vingt Masques grotesques, before 1888 (CB 409)
Etchings and softground cut out and printed by the artist: three masks on the same sheet, 24.9 x 33.2 cm (sheet size)
Bibliothèque Nationale, D. 99996; Ef 477, t. XI.

89b *Twenty Grotesque Masks*
Vingt Masques grotesques, before 1888 (CB 409)
Etchings and softground cut out and printed by the artist: three masks on the same sheet, 25.2 x 32.6 cm (sheet size)
Signed: lr artist's monogram
Bibliothèque Nationale, D. 99996; Ef 477, t. XI.

90a *Foliage of Water Lilies*
Feuillage d'eau aux nénuphars, c. 1887 (CB 417)
Etching, softground, and aquatint, 41.3 x 27.4 cm
Signed: lr in pencil "H. Guérard," on plate mark "État d'essai superposition de 2 planches. Épreuve unique," lc artist's monogram
Bibliothèque Nationale, D. 99996; Ef 477, t. XI.

90b *Foliage of Water Lilies*
Feuillage d'eau aux nénuphars, c. 1887 (CB 417)
Etching, roulette, softground, and aquatint touched with gold, 41.3 x 27.4 cm
Signed: lr in plate " H. Guérard"
Bibliothèque Nationale, D. 99996; Ef 477, t. XI.

91 *Fisherman with Plaice*
Le Pêcheur au carrelet, before 1892 (CB 200—II)
Etching, softground, aquatint and scraper, 26.5 x 17.9 cm
Signed: lr in plate "H. Guérard," lc in pencil "planche poncée et trait remordu 2ème état Épreuve unique H. Guérard," lc artist's monogram in gold ink
Bibliothèque Nationale, D. 99996; Ef 477, t. V.

92 A Pontoon, Venice
Un Ponton d'embarquement, Venise, 1893 (CB 207—I)
Etching and softground, 31.1 x 38.4 cm
Signed: ll in pencil "1er état tiré à 4 par l'auteur no.
4 H. Guérard," ll artist's monogram
Bibliothèque Nationale, D. 99996; Ef 477, t. V.

Paul HELLEU (1859-1927)
Born in Vannes (Morbihan), Paul Helleu entered the École des Beaux-Arts in 1876 and became connected with Whistler, Stevens, Sargent, Monet, and Rodin. He began etching in 1885 and, like his friend Tissot, etched with a diamond point. With Comte Robert de Montesquiou-Fezensac he frequented the salons of the aristocratic and literary world; he found his models there. Some of his etchings, with editions of not more than ten, are printed à la poupée (The Hat with Feathers, Liane de Pougy, Profile of Mademoiselle Hamoir, Portrait of Madeleine Carlier, and the surprising Hydrangeas, created around 1896). A successful painter and etcher (Goncourt painted his portrait and he appeared as the character of Elstir in À la recherche du temps perdu), he was well received in England and in the United States. He was less active in etching after 1912. M. G.

93 Hydrangeas
Les Hortensias, c. 1896
*Drypoint, touched with golden bronze and purple, 33.1 x 43.2 cm
Signed: ll in pencil "Helleu"
Bibliothèque Nationale, D. 10485 (Mme. Howard-Johnston, 23 September 1957); Ef 431, t. I.

94 Portrait of Madeleine Carlier
Portrait de Madeleine Carlier, c. 1904 (IFF 403)
*Drypoint, 54.9 x 33.3 cm
Signed: ll in pencil "Helleu"
Bibliothèque Nationale, D. 7374 (legs A. Curtis, no. 18-72, 26 October 1949); Ef 431, t. V.

Charles-Marie-Louis HOUDARD
(active between 1892 and 1914)
A pupil of Lefebvre and Boulanger, Charles Houdard began etching in color in 1894: Frogs and Iris, a color etching of Japanese inspiration, was published during that year in L'Estampe Originale. At the 1895 Salon he presented Frogs and Rushes and Capucines. He exhibited again in 1896 and 1897. In October-November 1898 he published Travel Impressions, a series of ten color prints in an edition of twenty-five, including The Meuse at Dordrecht, Mills at Dordrecht, The Heights of Crozon, The Old Jetties at Tréport, Moonlight on the Bresle, On the Bresle, At Tréport, The Lake, Frogs and Iris, Frogs and Rushes, and Capucines. He attended the first Salon of the Société de la Gravure Originale en Couleurs with six works, all printed in editions of 100 and sold for 50 francs: three views of The Villa d'Este, The Church of Sainte-Françoise-Romaine, The Basilica of Constantine, and The Temple of Castor and Pollux. He exhibited at the Salon until 1912, and was represented by Georges Petit. In 1905 Jacques Doucet bought two of his works, The Dune and The Expanse of Water (editions of 200, 80 francs). M. G.

95 Frogs and Iris
Grenouilles et Iris, 1894 (IFF 1)
Aquatint, 26 x 40 cm
Signed: lr in pencil "no. 34/Ch. Houdard," ur in image artist's monogram, ll blind stamp of L'Estampe Originale
Zimmerli Art Museum, David A. and Mildred H. Morse Art Acquisition Fund.

96 Capucines, 1898 (IFF 3)
Etching and aquatint, 30.5 x 22.9 cm
Signed: lr in pencil "no. 4/Ch. Houdard," lr artist's monogram in red ink
(Tenth plate of a series of ten color prints from Impressions de voyage, an edition of twenty-five, published by the artist)
Bibliothèque Nationale, D. 9370 (Ch. Hessèle, 29 May 1899); Ef 509.

97 End of Day
Fin de jour, before 1901 (IFF 7)
Aquatint and softground, 23.8 x 34.6 cm
Signed: lr in pencil "no. 13/15/Ch. Houdard," ll "Fin de jour"
Bibliothèque Nationale, D. 712 (Ch. Houdard, 13 February 1908); Ef 509.

Francisco ITURRINO (1864-1924)
After studying in Belgium, Iturrino arrived in Paris in 1895 where he studied at the Académie Julian along with the Belgian Henri Evenepoel and Henri Matisse. By the turn of the century he was well integrated in the young Spanish avant-garde community, which included Canals, Sunyer, and eventually Picasso, all living at the Bateau-Lavoir in Montmartre. Iturrino must have visited the studio of the etcher and printer Eugène Delâtre to obtain technical knowledge of the highly textural, tonal, and abstract application of acid in the production of color etchings. P. D. C.

98 Women in the Wood
Les femmes dans le bois, c. 1900
*Etching and aquatint, 39.6 x 48.3 cm
Signed: lr in pencil "F. Iturrino"
Zimmerli Art Museum, Mindy and Ramon Tublitz Purchase Fund.

99 The Outdoor Concert
Le concert champêtre, c. 1900
*Etching and aquatint, 34 x 43.8 cm
Signed: lr in pencil "F. Iturrino"
Zimmerli Art Museum.

Pierre-Georges JEANNIOT (1848-1934)
Born in Geneva, Pierre-Georges Jeanniot was the son of the director of the École des Beaux-Arts in Dijon, who was also the teacher of Legrand. He made his first etching in 1877. He tried almost every technique: wood and lithography from 1892; monotype in 1890 (the idea came from Count Lepic, and he experimented with it with his friend Degas); and of course etching (he printed on his own manual press, following Lepère's advice, but came to require the help of professional printers such as Maire in 1905, and undoubtedly Delâtre). An admirer of Rembrandt, Corot, and Degas, Jeanniot claimed never to

work without a model, but did work from memory and found a greater freedom of execution in the color etchings which he produced from 1900. Woman in a Rocking Chair, Polo, On the Beach, Sada Yacco, and The Milliners demonstrate the talent of an artist known mainly for his illustrations and for his series of engravings portraying the atrocities of World War I, but who also produced some of the most accomplished etchings au repérage, sometimes highlighted à la poupée (On the Beach). Polo, an etching printed in its first state to produce five proofs, was sold for 50 francs by Charles Hessèle in 1899. Reworked with aquatint, and printed in an edition of twenty-five, it was presented at the Decennal and was noticed by the critic of La Plume on August 1, 1900. The Bibliothèque Nationale's print is dedicated to Béjot and shows which artists influenced Jeanniot in color etching. Jeanniot was represented at the Salons of 1901 (The Milliners and Women in White), 1904 (Lydie and The Amateur), and 1905 (Polo—the plate belonged to the Société des Amis de l'Eau-Forte from 1904), and participated in the first Salon of la Gravure Originale en Couleurs with The Amateur (edition of 100, 75 francs) and two illustrations. In 1908 he presented four works: Five O'Clock, The Head Scarf, The Walk, and The Restaurant (all editions of 200, 50 to 80 francs). In 1909 he exhibited At the Restaurant and The Paddock (editions of 200, 80 francs), achieving great commercial success without compromising his talent. Praised by Manet, Degas and Pissarro, he was also recognized by Jacques Doucet. M. G.

100 Polo
Le Polo, c. 1899 (IFF 53)
Etching and aquatint, 30 x 39.5 cm
Signed: ll in pencil "Jeanniot/à son ami Béjot," lr in pencil "tir. 25 ép. no. 4," lr artist's monogram
(Reproduced in G. Mourey, "Coloured Etchings in France," The Studio, XXII, 1901)
Bibliothèque Nationale, A. 3570; Dc 392a, t. II.

101 Woman in a Rocking Chair
La Femme au rocking-chair, 1900 (IFF 41)
Softground, etching, and aquatint, 29.9 x 39.7 cm
Signed: ll in pencil "Jeanniot," lr in pencil "tir. 25 no. 25," lr artist's monogram
Bibliothèque Nationale, A. 9165 (G. Jeanniot, 14 June 1933); Dc 392a, t. I.

102 On the Beach
Sur la plage, c. 1900 (IFF 55)
Etching, drypoint, and aquatint, touched with red, 23 x 33 cm
Signed: ll in pencil "Jeanniot," lr in pencil "tir. 25 ép. no. 10," lr artist's monogram
(Reproduced in G. Mourey, "Coloured Etchings in France," The Studio, XXII, 1901)
Bibliothèque Nationale, A. 9165; Dc 392a, t. II.

Francis JOURDAIN (1876-1958)
The son of writer, architect, and art critic Frantz Jourdain, Francis Jourdain was introduced to the process of color etching by Eugène Delâtre in the first half of the 1890s. In 1896 Jourdain was represented by a color etching at an exhibition at Le Barc de Boutteville and in 1898 exhibited color etchings

187

with Eugène Delâtre at the Durand-Ruel gallery; he also participated in the first Salon of the Société de la Gravure Originale en Couleurs in 1904. Jourdain associated with the young Parisian avant-garde who took part in the productions of the Théâtre de l'Œuvre, and was responsible for introducing Villon to color etching. P. D. C.

103 | *Woman in the Shade*
Femme dans l'ombre, c. 1900
Aquatint, 53.5 x 39 cm
Signed: lr in pencil "40 ép. no. 7/Francis Jourdain"
Zimmerli Art Museum, Mindy and Ramon Tublitz Purchase Fund.

104 | *The Sea*
La Mer, c. 1900
Etching and aquatint, 41.5 x 32 cm
Signed: lr in ink "30 épr. no. 23," "Francis Jourdain," ll in pencil "509," lr monogram M.N.
Bibliothèque Nationale, D. 3302 (Musée du Luxembourg, 2 April 1931); AA3 Jourdain.

Elisabeth KROUGLICOFF (1865-1941)
Having studied at the Moscow School of Painting, Sculpture and Architecture under Konstantin Alexeievich Korovin (1861-1939) and others, Krouglicoff settled in Paris in 1895 and remained there until her return to Russia at the outbreak of World War I. Her studio on the rue Boissonade in Montparnasse was a center for Russian artists and writers. In Paris she studied at the Académie Vitty and the Académie Colarossi. She produced her first etching in 1902, and the following year she created a series of portraits of children in the media of drypoint, softground, and aquatint; in general, however, her subjects were landscapes and cityscapes in muted colors. Krouglicoff printed her etchings herself à la poupée from zinc plates in editions of twenty-five to thirty, often with a painterly wiping of ink on the plate. In 1904 she became a member of the Société de la Gravure Originale en Couleurs. P. D. C.
[E.S. *Krouglicoff, Life and Art*, ed. P. E. Kornilov, (Leningrad, 1969) in Russian]

105 | *The Silver Birches*
Les Bouleaux, c. 1902
*Aquatint and monotype, 23.7 x 33.9 cm
Signed: lr in pencil "E. Krouglicoff," ll in pencil "Les Bouleaux/Épreuve d'essai."
Zimmerli Art Museum, David A. and Mildred H. Morse Art Acquisition Fund.

Marie LAURENCIN (1883-1956)
Having studied at the Académie Humbert, boulevard de Clichy (where she met Braque and Picabia, who was producing his first color etching), Marie Laurencin in 1907 became a part of the group of artists and poets who frequented the Bateau-Lavoir in Montmartre: Picasso, Braque, Marcoussis, Derain, MacOrlan, Valéry Larbaud, and Guillaume Appollinaire (indeed she became the driving force behind the latter). Around 1904 she began to experiment in etching under the influence of Laboureur: her first plates were aquatints, etchings, and the occasional woodcut, depicting the symbolic female figures Salome

or Bilitis. As in her painting, her main preoccupation was color. "Mlle Laurencin's personality trembles with joy, purity is her domain, in it she develops freely," wrote Appollinaire in *La Revue des Lettres et des Arts* (May 1, 1908). Although she produced many etchings and aquatints (seventy-one between 1904 and 1956), and was aided in printing by Laboureur from 1904 to 1928, she is known principally for her color lithography. M. G.
[D. Marchesseau, *Catalogue Raisonné de l'œuvre gravé de Marie Laurencin* (Tokyo, 1981)]

106 | *The Songs of Bilitis*
Les Chansons de Bilitis, 1906 (M 1; IFF 1—III)
Drypoint and aquatint, 24 x 15 cm
Signed: lr in pencil "Marie Laurencin. Les chansons de Bilitis," ll in pencil "1906"
Bibliothèque Nationale, D. 4081 (Seymour de Ricci, 6 January 1936); Dc 433.

Louis LEGRAND (1863-1951)
A pupil of the École des Beaux-Arts in Dijon, Louis Legrand made a name for himself in Paris by contributing to the *Journal Amusant*, the *Chronique Parisienne*, and the *Courrier Français* (1887-84). His acute skills of observation, his hard lines softened by a few strokes of the paintbrush on the plate, and his often erotic or macabre subject matter featuring girls and dancers contributed to the success of an artist who in 1896—when he was only 32 years old—was the subject of a catalogue of etchings by Erastène Ramiro, an admirer and pupil of Rops. His success can be attributed to the scandal caused by etchings such as *Death on the Field of Honor* (1887), *Prostitution* (c. 1887), and *Naturalism*. Legrand became interested in color as early as 1887: *Industry and Sloth* was printed in sepia and blue, and *Woman with Umbrella* was printed à la poupée in blue and green. Siegfried Bing exhibited his work in 1896, and Georges Petit gave him a personal exhibition in 1904. That same year he participated in the first Salon of the Société de la Gravure Originale en Couleurs, of which he was a member, with *The Ancestress, Mistress, Maternal Bliss, Diners, Profiles, Illustration of Parisian Fauna, Breton Landscape, The Hetaira*, and *The Carpenter's Son* (mostly editions of seventy-five, 50 to 400 francs). This was the only time he exhibited with this society. At the 1904 Salon he presented *The Ancestress* and at the 1905 Salon, *The Parisian*. In July 1897 his publisher, Gustave Pellet, 51 rue Le Peletier, exhibited fourteen etchings, *The Little Ballet Girls* (edition of 100, 120 francs for the series). Publisher of Rops and Toulouse-Lautrec, Pellet produced over three hundred plates that were also distributed by his son-in-law Maurice Exsteens, author of an unpublished catalogue of Louis Legrand. M. G.
[*Catalogue des archives de la maison Gustave Pellet-Maurice Exsteens* (Bern: Klipstein & Kornfeld, 1962)]

107 | *Woman with Umbrella*
La Femme au parapluie, c. 1887 (E 17; IFF 21—IV)
*Etching, drypoint, and aquatint, 36.5 x 15.5 cm
Signed: ur in plate artist's monogram, lr in black crayon "Louis Legrand," lr red monogram G.P. (Gustave Pellet), ll "à la poupée 4e"
Bibliothèque Nationale, D. 11898 (M. Exsteens, 3 June 1960); Dc 375, t. I.

108a | *Industry and Sloth*
Le Travail et la Paresse, c. 1887 (E 14; IFF 17—VIII)
Etching, drypoint, aquatint and scraper in red, 37 x 21 cm
Signed: ul in plate "Le Travail/et la Paresse," ul artist's monogram, in green crayon "Louis Legrand"
Bibliothèque Nationale, D. 11898; Dc 375, t. I.

108b | *Industry and Sloth*
Le Travail et la Paresse, c. 1887 (E 14; IFF 17—IX)
*Etching, drypoint, aquatint and scraper in red and blue, 37 x 21 cm
Signed: ul in plate "Le Travail/et la Paresse," ul artist's monogram, lr in black crayon "Louis Legrand," lr monogram G.P. (Gustave Pellet, Lugt 1190)
Bibliothèque Nationale, D. 11898; Dc 375, t. I.

109 | *Return from the Shoot* or *The Pheasant*
Retour de chasse ou Le Faisan, c. 1892 (E 42; IFF 34)
*Aquatint, 15.5 x 26 cm
Signed: lr in pencil "à Pellet/Louis Legrand," lr red monogram, lr monogram G.P. (Gustave Pellet, Lugt 1190)
Bibliothèque Nationale, D. 11898; Dc 375, t. II.

110a | *The Idiot*
L'Idiot, c. 1895 (E 85; IFF 52—II)
*Etching and aquatint printed from cut-out plate and touched with yellow, 52 x 49.5 cm (sheet size)
Signed: in blue crayon "Louis Legrand," immediately below signature red monogram
Bibliothèque Nationale, D. 11898; Dc 375, t. V.

110b | *The Idiot and the Dancer*
L'Idiot et le Plié, c. 1895 (E 86; IFF 51 and 52)
Etching and aquatint printed from three copper plates, 53 x 32 cm (sheet size)
Signed: in plate "Eaux fortes/de/Louis Legrand," in pencil "L.L.," lr "L'Idiot et le plié," and red monogram
(Cover for series of etchings by Louis Legrand. Copper plates cut out for cover)
Bibliothèque Nationale, D. 11898; Dc 375, t. V.

Georges LEPAPE (1887-1971)
Painter, decorator, etcher and illustrator, Georges Lepape was taught by Humbert and then Cormon at the École des Beaux-Arts in 1902. He exhibited at the Salon des Indépendants and at various other Salons from 1904. His first monotypes and etchings (*Filling the Automobile, At the Seaside*) date from 1906. From 1910, encouraged by Paul Poiret, he illustrated *Les Choses de Paul Poiret* and contributed to various publications, including *La Gazette du Bon Ton, Fémina, Harper's Bazaar*, and *Vogue*. He created a new style for women inspired by *Persanes*, a play produced by Diaghilev, and had great influence upon the decorative arts of his era. The hallmarks of this artist were grace and elegance. M. G.

111 | *At the Seaside*
Au bord de la mer, 1906
Etching and aquatint, 16.2 x 20.2 cm
Signed: ll in plate "Georges Lepape," lc in pencil "État"
Zimmerli Art Museum, David A. and Mildred H. Morse Art Acquisition Fund.

Louis-Auguste LEPÈRE (1849-1918)

Best known as a prolific wood-engraver and an advocate of original printmaking, Lepère officially began his career in 1875 as a reproductive wood-engraver for the journals *Le Monde illustré* and *Le Magasin pittoresque*. By the early 1880s new photomechanical printing processes had made the role of the reproductive wood-engraver obsolete; Lepère therefore concentrated more and more on promoting wood-engraving as an original printmaking process; these activities culminated in 1888 with his founding of the Société de l'Estampe Originale and the publication of his first album *L'Estampe Originale*, comprising ten black-and-white prints in various media. This was followed the next year by a second album including Henri Boutet's hand-colored etching *Punchinello*. It was not until 1893, when André Marty acquired from Lepère the right to use the title *L'Estampe Originale* and began publishing his own albums under that name, that Lepère, with Eugène Delâtre as his teacher, created two of the total of three color etchings in his oeuvre. *The Washerwomen*, printed in an edition of 100 for Marty's third album of *L'Estampe Originale*, followed *Summer* (L-B 81), an edition of thirty; four years later Lepère was commissioned by the Société des Amis des Arts de Bordeaux to create *Landing Stage on the Garonne, Bordeaux*, an edition of twenty-five. P. D. C.

[A. Lotz-Brissonneau, *L'Oeuvre gravé d'Auguste Lepère* (Paris, 1905)]

112 The Washerwomen
Blanchisseuses (Jeunesse passe vite vertu !...) 1893 (L-B 91)
Softground, etching, and aquatint, 38.1 x 20.9 cm
Signed: lr in plate in blue pencil "A. Lepère," ul in plate "Jeunesse pass vite vertu!...," ll blind stamp of *L'Estampe Originale*
Zimmerli Art Museum, Class of 1944 Art Purchase Fund.

113 Landing Stage on the Garonne, Bordeaux
Embarcadère sur la Garonne, Bordeaux, 1897 (L-B 106)
Etching and aquatint, 27.9 x 34.2 cm
Signed: ll "A. Lepère/97"
Zimmerli Art Museum, David A. and Mildred H. Morse Art Acquisition Fund.

Maxime MAUFRA (1861-1918)

Maxime Maufra was a pupil of illustrator and engraver Edmond Chazerain at the Lycée de Nantes and in 1879 studied under Alfred Leduc and Charles Lebourg. Painter above all (he exhibited at the 1886 Salon and participated in an important exhibition in Nantes), Maufra frequented Pont-Aven and Le Pouldu, and in 1890-91 met Henry Moret and visited Paul Gauguin with Émile Dezaunay. In 1892 he moved to Paris, to Place Ravignon at the foot of Montmartre. He visited Eugène Delâtre's workshop and discovered etching. In 1893 he experimented with lithography at Edward Ancourt's workshop: *The Road to Gaud*, his first lithography, was printed in color by Ancourt. Although he worked readily in color lithography, it was not until 1908 that he produced his only color etching, *Château de Lavardin*, printed in sanguine. M. G.

[Daniel Morane, *Maxime Maufra 1861-1918. Catalogue raisonné de l'œuvre gravé* (Musée de Pont-Aven, 1986)]

114 Château de Lavardin, 1908 (M 49)
Etching in sanguine, 14.8 x 19.6 cm
Signed: lr in ink "Maufra 1908," lr in plate "1908"
Bibliothèque Nationale, Dc 525.

Charles MAURIN (1856-1914)

Maurin studied at the Académie Julian from 1875-79. Through his continued contact with the Académie Julian and his participation in the Salon des Indépendants during the 1880s, he became associated with the emerging avant-garde of the 1890s such as Toulouse-Lautrec and members of the Nabis. A prolific and experimental printmaker, Maurin created around two hundred prints during his career, of which more than a hundred were color etchings. Working with Eugène Delâtre in 1890-91, Maurin perfected a system of color etching from multiple plates; along with Guérard, Raffaëlli, Cassatt, and Pissarro, he was an initiator of the color etching movement. Published by Sagot, Vollard, and Hessèle, Maurin's prints were brought to public attention by Gustave Pellet, who published such albums as *Sentimental Education* (1896) and *Little Class* (1897), as well as many individual color images. Using various qualities of aquatint grains and burnishing them down, Maurin sought to produce varieties and subtleties of texture and color rarely achieved in printmaking before. In 1898 Maurin fought for the admission of color prints to the annual Salon of the reactionary Société des Artistes Français, whose print section consisted mainly of reproductive engravings and had been closed to color prints since 1891. The next year color prints were reluctantly admitted to the Salon; yet by then the official Salon had become an archaic institution, and artists had found alternative means to promote their art. P. D. C.

[Maurice Fréchuret, *L'Œuvre de Charles Maurin. Un symbolisme du réel*, History of Art doctoral thesis, University of Lyon II, 1986, 4 vols.]

115 The Card Player
La Tireuse des cartes, 1891 (F 664)
Etching and aquatint, 18.2 x 13 cm
Signed: lr in plate signature and date
Zimmerli Art Museum, David A. and Mildred H. Morse Art Acquisition Fund.

116 Nude
Nu, 1891
Etching, aquatint, and drypoint, 38.2 x 32 cm
Signed: ul in plate in reverse "Ch. Maurin 1891"
Zimmerli Art Museum, David A. and Mildred H. Morse Art Acquisition Fund.

117 Woman and Cat
Une Femme et un chat, 1891 (F 590)
Etching and aquatint touched with watercolor, 15.4 x 18.8 cm
Signed: ll in plate artist's monogram
Zimmerli Art Museum, David A. and Mildred H. Morse Art Acquisition Fund.

118 Young Girl on a Bench, Sewing
Jeune Fille cousant sur un banc, 1891-92 (F 614)
Softground, etching, and aquatint, 27.3 x 22 cm
Signed: ll Sagot blind stamp, ll in pencil "Jeune fille cousant dans un square"
(The title is the one used by Sagot in the sale catalogue of September 1892, no. 34)
Zimmerli Art Museum, Friends Purchase Fund.

119 Young Woman in a Park, Sewing
Jeune Femme cousant dans un jardin public, 1890-92 (F 615)
Softground, 27.2 x 22.2 cm
Signed: lr in thick pencil "Maurin"
Bibliothèque Nationale, former collection of Henry Laurent no. 862; A. 67272 (19 April 1977); Dc 617, t. II.

120a Montmartre with View of Paris
Montmartre avec vue de Paris, c. 1900 (F 616)
Etching and aquatint in blue, 26.7 x 49.2 cm
Signed: lr in pencil "Maurin"
Zimmerli Art Museum, David A. and Mildred H. Morse Art Acquisition Fund.

120b Montmartre with View of Paris
Montmartre avec vue de Paris, c. 1900 (F 616)
Etching and aquatint, 26.7 x 49.2 cm
Signed: lr in pencil "Maurin"
Zimmerli Art Museum, gift of Marion and Allan Maitlin.

121 Bathroom
Salle de bains, n.d. (F 545)
*Drypoint, roulette, and aquatint, 23.4 x 20 cm
Signed: lr in pencil "Maurin"
Bibliothèque Nationale, D. 8716; Dc 617, t. I.

122 Man and Woman Undressing
Homme et Femme se déshabillant, n.d. (F 742)
Sprayed aquatint and softground, 20 x 16 cm
Signed: ll in plate "Maurin," lr in pencil "Maurin"
Bibliothèque Nationale, D. 8716 (Charles Laurent, 24 June 1953); Dc 617, t. I.

123 Intimacy
Intimité, n.d. (F 570)
Aquatint, 20 x 15.1 cm
Signed: in pencil "Maurin"
Bibliothèque Nationale, A. 1988—74462; Dc 617, t. I.

Ferdinand MICHL (1877-?)

Little is known about Michl except that he studied in Prague and Munich, worked in Vienna, and often visited Paris; in 1905 he exhibited a color etching entitled *The Théâtre Marigny* at the Salon of the Société Nationale des Beaux-Arts. The economic but dramatic use of color aquatint and the *demi-monde* subject matter of *At the Café* relate specifically to the work of Villon. P. D. C.

124 At the Café
Au Café, 1900
*Etching and aquatint, 29.9 x 26.2 cm
Signed: ul in plate "Ferd Michl/Paris 1900," lr in pencil "Ferd Michl/Paris," ll artist's monogram, ll in pencil "4/20"
Zimmerli Art Museum, gift of Marion and Allan Maitlin.

Victor MIGNOT (1872-1944)
In the early 1890s, this Belgian artist-illustrator worked for the journal *Belgian Cycling*; moving back and forth between Brussels and Paris, Mignot produced the poster for the fifth Salon de Cycle in Brussels in 1897 and illustrated two covers of the Paris art and literary journal *Cocorico* in 1899. In 1903 Mignot was living in Paris, but was also included in the annual exhibition organized by Le Sillon, an artistic society in Brussels. As a member of the Société de la Gravure Originale en Couleurs, he was represented by ten prints, including *The Trinket*, in the society's fourth Salon and by four in its fifth Salon in 1908. P. D. C.

125　*The Trinket*
Le Bibelot, 1907
Aquatint, 46 x 33 cm
Signed: lr in plate "V. Mignot," ll in pencil "30/100," ll blind stamp "R. Marc—Dardonville, Paris"
Zimmerli Art Museum, Mindy and Ramon Tublitz Purchase Fund.

Alfredo MÜLLER (1869-1939)
After studying painting in Florence, Müller moved to Paris with his parents in 1888 where he continued his studies with renowned academic painters such as François Flameng and Carolus Duran. By the turn of the century Müller was exhibiting regularly at the Salon of the Société Nationale des Beaux-Arts, and he was represented at the 1906 exhibition of the Société de la Gravure Originale en Couleurs. Beginning in 1897 and continuing over the next decade, probably under the instruction of Eugène Delâtre, Müller produced about a hundred color etchings. In 1899 Müller's *Two Girls Playing in a Garden* was included in *Germinal*, a series of twenty prints in various media published by La Maison Moderne in an edition of 100 with a preface by Gustave Geoffroy. While not included in Gabriel Mourey's 1901 article on color etching, Müller's work in the medium was highlighted by Mourey in the 1902 special issue of *The Studio* entitled "Modern Etching and Engraving." Fourteen of his color etchings, published by the dealer Pierrefort, were reproduced in *Le Courrier Français* between February and November 1904. Much of Müller's work combines densely bitten aquatint grain and irregularly wiped plates, epitomizing the turn-of-the-century predilection in color etching for rich painterly effects, often dark, abstract, and expressing an ambiguous mood. Unlike Steinlen, Sunyer, Bottini, and Villon, but like Robbe and Mignot, Müller avoided controversial and socially critical subjects and aimed his work at a bourgeois market. P. D. C.

126　*Two Girls Playing in a Garden*
Deux Fillettes jouant dans un jardin, 1899
*Aquatint and monotype, 43.8 x 43.8 cm
Signed: lr in crayon "Müller no. 70"
(Published in the album *Germinal*)
Zimmerli Art Museum.

127　*Suzanne Despres in Poil de Carotte*
Suzanne Despres dans Poil de Carotte, c. 1900
*Aquatint, 48.5 x 32.5 cm
Signed: ur in plate "Suzanne Despres dans Poil de Carotte," lr in pencil "Müller," ll in pencil "no. 24," lr in blue crayon "A Monsieur Y. Calella avec les amitiés de Madame Despres"
Zimmerli Art Museum, gift of Harold and Barbara Kaplan.

128　*Portrait of Woman with Straw Hat*
Portrait de femme au chapeau de paille, c.1900
*Etching, aquatint, and monotype, 44.4 x 35.5 cm
Signed: ll in plate "Müller"
Zimmerli Art Museum, David A. and Mildred H. Morse Art Acquisition Fund.

129　*At the Moulin Rouge*
Au Moulin-Rouge, c. 1900
Etching and aquatint, 35.5 x 33.5 cm
Signed: ll in plate "Müller," ll in pencil "no. 44," "Müller"
Zimmerli Art Museum, Class of 1937 Art Purchase Fund.

130　*Recreation*
La Récréation, c. 1900
Etching, 18.4 x 14.8 cm
Signed: lr in ink "Müller," ll in crayon, "No. 15"
Zimmerli Art Museum, Class of 1937 Art Purchase Fund.

131　*Montmartre, rue Saint-Vincent in Winter*
Rue à Montmartre ou Montmartre, la rue St Vincent en hiver, c. 1900
*Etching and aquatint touched with pigment, 37.2 x 25 cm
Signed: lr in plate "Müller," lr in pencil "Müller 33/40"
Zimmerli Art Museum.

132　*Fishing Fleet*
Flotille de bateau pêcheurs, 1902
*Etching and aquatint, 39.7 x 49.5 cm
Signed: lr in plate "Müller 1902," lr in pencil "Müller," "Essai no. 1," ul in pencil "Tirée une épreuve nature essuyée main et retroussée du ton du ciel"
Zimmerli Art Museum, David A. and Mildred H. Morse Art Acquisition Fund.

Pablo Ruiz PICASSO (1881-1973)
In 1899, Picasso and Ricardo Canals began to use the etching technique in Barcelona. Picasso showed his interest in it by producing *El Zurdo*, which depicts a left-handed picador. Five years later *The Frugal Repast* was the result of his experiments. Picasso came to Paris for the first time in October 1900 with his friend Carles Casagemas and settled for two months in the studio of another Catalan artist, Isidro Nonell, in the heart of Montmartre, 49 rue Gabrielle. Although he continued to travel between Paris and Barcelona, he gradually integrated into the "Catalan Montmartre" and the French avant-garde community, and finally settled in the Bateau-Lavoir in Spring 1904. Picasso probably worked with Canals again, this time in Eugène Delâtre's atelier. The latter was in charge of printing the first edition of *The Frugal Repast*, as well as the famous proofs pulled in blue-green. P. D. C.
[B. Geiser, *Picasso, peintre-graveur: catalogue illustré de l'œuvre gravé et lithographié, 1899-1931* (Bern: 1933, 2nd ed. 1955)]

133　*The Frugal Repast*
Le Repas Frugal, 1904
Etching in blue, 46 x 38 cm
Signed: r "Picasso"
The Art Institute of Chicago, Clarence Buckingham Collection.
(This work is exhibited only in New Brunswick)

134　*Standing Nude I*
Nu debout I, 1906-07 (G 19)
Drypoint in red, 22.9 x 15 cm
Musée Picasso.
(This work is exhibited only in Amsterdam and Paris)

135　*Standing Nude II*
Nu debout II, 1906-07 (G 20)
Drypoint in red, 22.9 x 15 cm
Musée Picasso.
(This work is exhibited only in Amsterdam and Paris)

Joseph-Porphyre PINCHON (1871-1953)
A pupil of Cormon, Pinchon exhibited at the Société Nationale des Beaux-Arts from 1904 and became a member in 1908. He was published by Georges Petit. M.G.

136　*Dog*
Chien, c. 1900
Aquatint, 22.2 x 29.5 cm
Signed: lr in pencil "Pinchon," ll in pencil "2e État. Tiré à 25"
Zimmerli Art Museum, gift of Frederick Mezey and Lucinda Porter Mezey.

Camille PISSARRO (1830-1903)
Of all the Impressionists, Pissarro was the most interested in experimenting with printmaking. "They are only etched impressions," he said of his works, usually pulling only a few proofs. His first color prints were in monotype, a technique which he began to pursue with Degas in 1878-79. But he began to experiment with color etching and aquatint in 1879, printing the eighth proof of *Dusk with Haystacks* in Van Dyck brown on the back of the invitation to the wedding of Louis Gonse (like Pissarro, Gonse was an admirer of Japanese civilization). Other proofs, also monochrome, were printed in green or blue. Only in 1894 did he really begin to use color: *Church and Farm at Éragny* was printed from four plates *au repérage*. The Bibliothèque Nationale still holds the copper plates for this work; they came from C. Servant, planisher, 45 rue des Grands Augustins. It also holds the steel-faced plates for *Little Peasant Girls in the Grass*, *Market at Gisors (rue de Cappeville)*, and *Bathing Goosegirls*, all printed in color, only a few proofs of each, by Pissarro himself in 1894-95 on the press that he bought from Eugène Delâtre. In Pissarro's letter to Vollard of June 18, 1896, it is evident that he did not intend to sell his proofs straightaway but hoped to produce more. While he railed against color lithographs—"the exaggeration of complementary tones," "the pretty color"—he also tried to "find just the right colors," similar to Mary Cassatt but in a different mode. "It is touching up, and that is all," he wrote to Lucien on January 18, 1895. Vollard exhibited

several of Camille Pissarro's works in June 1896. A hard-working artist, always ready to undertake new research, Pissarro strove for success but without compromising his principles: this is why he refused to sell his color etchings separately, keeping them for a hypothetical album that he never completed. He insisted on selling his work at high prices when he should have made allowances for the depressed market, and so he disheartened his dealers. In November 1897 he seemed to be on the point of finalizing an arrangement with Eugène Rodrigues—otherwise known as Erastène Ramiro—who had just founded a society for the publication of etchings. But, while Mary Cassatt, Legrand, Ranft, Eugène Delâtre, Villon, Sunyer, and Maurin contributed to L'Estampe moderne from October 1897, there is no trace of work by Pissarro in this publication. He did make contact with Hessèle in 1897 and with Joyant in 1898; it is therefore not true to say that Pissarro had no commercial aims in printmaking. However, he sought more to accomplish his work in his own way than to please the public. M. G.
[Loÿs Delteil, Le Peintre-Graveur illustré, vol. XVII (1923)]
[Jean Leymarie, Michel Melot, Les Gravures des impressionnistes Manet, Pissarro, Renoir, Cézanne, Sisley (Paris, 1971)]

[137] *Dusk with Haystacks*
Crépuscule avec Meules, 1879 (LD 23—III; LM 22)
Etching and aquatint in Van Dyck brown, printed on back of invitation to the marriage of Louis Gonse and Anna Ellissen on 17 June 1879, 12.2 x 18 cm
Signed: ll in pencil "No. 8/Épreuve d'artiste/ Essai de Crépuscule," lr "C. Pissarro/Imp. par E Degas," and "brun Vandyck," lr monogram M.N.
Bibliothèque Nationale, Dc 419, t. I.

[138] *The Beggars*
Les Mendiantes, 1890-91 (LD 110—II; LM 111)
Etching and aquatint printed by Lucien Pissarro, 20 x 15.2 cm
Signed: ll artist's monogram "C.P.," lr "No. 1/II"
Bibliothèque Nationale, D. 3187 (Lucien, Paul, Georges, Ludovic-Rodolphe Pissarro, A. Bonin, 17 March 1930); Dc 419, t. III.

[139] *Church and Farm at Éragny*
Église et ferme à Éragny, 1894 (LD 96; LM 91)
Etching printed from four plates by Lucien Pissarro, 15.7 x 24.6 cm
Signed: ll artist's monogram "C.P.," lr "No. 1/II"
Bibliothèque Nationale, D. 3187; Dc 419, t. III.

[140a] *Little Peasant Girls in the Grass*
Paysannes à l'herbe, c. 1894 (LD 111; LM 113)
Etching and aquatint from four plates, 12 x 15 cm
Signed: ll in pencil "No. 8 ép. d'art./Paysannes à l'herbe," lr "C. Pissarro," lr monogram M.N.
Bibliothèque Nationale, Dc 419, t. III.

[140b] *Little Peasant Girls in the Grass*
Paysannes à l'herbe, c. 1894 (LD 111; LM 113)
Etching and aquatint printed by Lucien Pissarro, 12 x 15 cm
Signed: ll artist's monogram "C.P.," lr "No. 1/II"
Bibliothèque Nationale, D. 3187 (Lucien, Paul, Georges, Ludovic-Rodolphe Pissarro, A. Bonin, 17 March 1930); Dc 419, t. III.

[141] *Market at Gisors (rue de Cappeville)*
Le Marché de Gisors (rue de Cappeville), c. 1894 (LD 112—VII; LM 112)
Etching from four plates (LD 144 b-e), 20 x 14.2 cm
Signed: ll in pencil "No. 4 Ép. d'art./Marché de Gisors (rue de Cappeville)", lr in pencil "C. Pissarro," lr in ink "en 4 planches," lr monogram M.N.
Bibliothèque Nationale, Dc 419, t. IV.

[142] *Bathing Goosegirls*
Baigneuses gardeuses d'oies, c. 1895 (LD 119—IX; LM 114)
Etching from four plates, 11.8 x 17.6 cm
Signed: ll in pencil "No. 9 ép. d'art./Baigneuses gardeuses d'oies," lr in pencil "C. Pissarro," ll in ink "en 4 planches," lr in pencil "Trait-Terre V-j. mars-bl. et peu de noir," lr monogram M.N.
Bibliothèque Nationale, Dc 419, t. IV.

Louis POTTER (dates unknown)

While L'Estampe et l'Affiche (May 15, 1899) lists seventeen etchings (fifteen in color) by Potter on sale at Hessèle's shop, and while Mourey mentions Potter in his article on color etching, we have, unfortunately, not been able to uncover further information on this artist. Mourey grouped Potter with artists such as Ranft, Maurin, and Jourdain who had experimented, à la Degas, in creating monotypes. L'Estampe et l'Affiche mentions a black-and-white etching measuring 18 x 13 cm entitled Man with Pipe but, although the subject is similar, its measurements do not match those of the color etching included here. P. D. C.

[143] *Seated Man*
Homme assis, c. 1900
*Aquatint, 35.6 x 26.8 cm
Signed: ll in pencil "Louis Potter," lr in pencil "tiré à 50—2"
Zimmerli Art Museum, Herbert Littman Purchase Fund.

Jean-François RAFFAËLLI (1850-1924)

Jean-François Raffaëlli was born in Paris. After a difficult start in life, he spent three months in 1870 in the studio of Jean-Léon Gérôme at the École des Beaux-Arts. Also in this year he was included for the first time in the Salon with a forest landscape. He was refused in 1872, but was not discouraged. A friend of Degas, he exhibited with the Impressionists in 1880 and 1881 and had established himself by the age of thirty. In 1884 he was producing his work in a boutique in avenue de l'Opéra. He painted portraits (Clémenceau, Edmond de Goncourt), landscapes, bouquets of flowers, but above all he focused on humble people, beggars and ragmen. He experimented with lithography and drypoint in 1876 and with color etching in 1889 but, as he stated in 1907, was not satisfied with the results. In 1897 Boussod-Valadon bought six plates from him and published them under the title Types of Simple Folk. The same year Raffaëlli contributed a color drypoint, Self-Portrait, to André Marty's L'Estampe Originale. At the 1894 Salon of the Société Nationale des Beaux-Arts he exhibited seven color etchings, several of which were engraved entirely with drypoint hatching and printed from five plates. In 1898

he organized the first exhibition of color etchings, including thirty by himself, at Bing's gallery. He became president of the Société de la Gravure Originale en Couleurs and held Salons at the Georges Petit gallery from 1904. The June 1907 catalogue included three color etchings, The Snow, The Storm, and The Little Donkeys (editions of 200, 44 x 56 cm, 100 francs); in 1908 it included The Boulevard des Italiens and The Old Oak (editions of 200, 44 x 57 cm, 125 francs). In 1906 the Société Nationale des Beaux-Arts asked him to organize an exhibition of color etchings. From November 25 to December 15, 1907 he held an exhibition of fifty-seven color prints at Devambez's gallery, 43 boulevard Malesherbes. Well-recognized in his time, Raffaëlli received a gold medal for his color etchings at the 1900 Universal Exhibition and, in 1909, was the subject of a major biography by Arsène Alexandre. M. G.
[Loÿs Delteil, Le Peintre-Graveur illustré, vol. XVI (Paris, 1923)]

[144] *Self-Portrait*
Autoportrait, 1893 (LD 7—II)
*Drypoint with retouching to eyes, nose, and mouth, 18.4 x 15.8 cm
Signed: lr "no. 101 JF Raffaëlli"
Bibliothèque Nationale, Dc 511.

[145] *The Seine at Asnières*
La Seine à Asnières, 1893 (LD 9—III)
*Drypoint and aquatint, 11.8 x 15.9 cm
Signed: in pencil "Épr. d'état/JF Raffaëlli"
Bibliothèque Nationale, D. 7374 (legs A. Curtis, 26 October 1949, no. 4288); Dc 511.

[146] *Breakfast*
Le Petit Déjeuner, 1895 (LD 26—II)
Etching and drypoint, 47 x 21 cm
Signed: lr in pencil "Ep. no. 8/JF Raffaëlli"
Zimmerli Art Museum, Herbert Littman Purchase Fund.

[147] *The Actress*
L'Actrice, 1898 (LD 51—II)
*Drypoint and aquatint, 35 x 26 cm
Signed: lr in image in pencil "1 à 60—Épreuve no. 47/JF Raffaëlli"
Bibliothèque Nationale, A. 9646 (P. Prouté, 20 June 1942); Dc 511.

[148] *Gentleman Having Just Painted His Gate*
Le Bonhomme venant de peindre sa barrière, 1904 (LD 55)
Drypoint, 26.5 x 19 cm
Signed: lr in pencil "no. 49/JF Raffaëlli"
Bibliothèque Nationale, A. 9646; Dc 511.

[149] *To Your Health: Mother Good Times!*
A Votre Santé: la mère Bontemps !, 1905 (LD 40—II)
Drypoint, 27 x 21.5 cm
Signed: lr in pencil "JF Raffaëlli," ll in pencil " no. 21"
Bibliothèque Nationale, D. 6102 (Mme. Chevrier de Beauchesne, 7 June 1946); Dc 511.

[150] *The Knife Grinder*
Le Rémouleur, 1907 (LD 76—II)
Drypoint, 22 x 46.5 cm
Signed: lr in pencil "Ep. No. 6/50/JF Raffaëlli"
Bibliothèque Nationale, D. 3302 (Musée du Luxembourg, 2 April 1931); Dc 511.

| 151 | Factories in the Snow

Les Usines sous la neige, 1909 (LD 89—II)
Etching and drypoint, 16 x 20 cm
Signed: lr in pencil "Ép No. 21, JF Raffaëlli"
Bibliothèque Nationale, D. 7374 (legs A. Curtis, 26 October 1949, no. 4291); Dc 511.

| 152 | Bust of Young Woman or The Little Milliner

Buste de jeune femme ou La Petite Modiste, n.d. (LD 117—I)
*Drypoint touched with black and red, 10.2 x 7.8 cm
Signed: lr in pencil "Ép. d'essai/JF Raffaëlli," lr in pencil "Pas de teinte grise" (the word "grise" is underlined three times)
Bibliothèque Nationale, A. 9646; Dc 511.

Richard RANFT (1862-1931)

Of Swiss origin, painter-etcher Richard Ranft was a pupil of Gustave Courbet, then in hiding in the tower of Peilz near Vevey. Ranft worked mostly in Paris. He produced occasional illustrations (Le Crépuscule des dieux by Élémir Bourges) and engravings after Fragonard, Watteau, Reynolds, Gainsborough, or Turner, but was known mainly for his color etchings. Sometimes verging on Symbolism—he participated in the first Salon de la Rose-Croix in 1892—Ranft's art was above all decorative and lyrical. His prints were produced in editions of twenty-five to fifty by Eugène Delâtre and published by Sagot. Some plates were never reprinted, for example the color etching The Swallow (only five proofs were pulled, and the plates were canceled). Others were made for albums, such as The Opera Ball, a color etching inked à la poupée in an edition of forty-five with five states, which appeared in the July 1899 edition of L'Estampe nouvelle. His entire oeuvre of etchings (eighty-five color etchings, six drypoints, two monotypes, one lithograph, twenty-six black-and-white etchings, sixteen etched interpretations in black-and-white and color) and various paintings, watercolors, gouaches, pastels, and fans were exhibited from June 8 to 25, 1910 at the Galérie des Artistes Modernes, 19 rue Caumartin, under the direction of J. Chaine and Simonson.
M. G.

| 153 | In the Box

Dans la Loge, c. 1899
*Drypoint, 34.5 x 24.8 cm
Signed: lr in plate "Richard Ranft," lr in pencil "Épreuve d'artiste/Richard Ranft," lr monogram M.N.
Bibliothèque Nationale, D. 3302 (Musée du Luxembourg, 2 April 1931); Ca 1c (xxe s.) Ranft.

| 154 | The Englishman at the Folies Bergères

L'Anglais aux Folies Bergères, 1899
*Etching and aquatint, 20 x 32.8 cm
Signed: lr "Épreuve tirée par l'artiste/Richard Ranft," lr monogram M.N.
Bibliothèque Nationale, D. 3302 (xxe s.) Ranft.

| 155a | Return from the Costume Ball

Le Retour du bal costumé, c. 1900
*Etching and aquatint, 30 x 38 cm
Signed: ll in ink "Richard Ranft," ll in pencil "no.

10," ll "hommage de l'auteur," lr monogram of the collector Ernest La Jeunesse
Zimmerli Art Museum.

| 155b | Return from the Costume Ball

Le Retour du bal costumé, c. 1900
*Etching and aquatint, 30 x 38 cm
Signed: ll "Richard Ranft," lr in pencil "No. 15/25 Richard Ranft," lr monogram of the collector Ernest La Jeunesse
Zimmerli Art Museum, Class of 1937 Art Purchase Fund.

| 156 | Morning Walk

Promenade matinale, c. 1900
*Etching and aquatint touched with watercolor, 58 x 25.4 cm
Signed: lr in plate "Richard Ranft," lr in pencil "Richard Ranft 9/50," ll in pencil "Promenade matinale"
Zimmerli Art Museum, Class of 1937 Art Purchase Fund.

| 157 | Polo

Le Polo, c. 1900
*Aquatint, 22 x 49.3 cm
Signed: ll in plate "Richard Ranft," lr in pencil "Épreuve d'artiste Richard Ranft," lr monogram M.N.
Bibliothèque Nationale, D. 3302; Ca 1c (xxe s.) Ranft.

| 158 | Haystacks in the Snow

Les Meules sous la neige, 1901
*Aquatint, 24.8 x 54.3 cm
Signed: lr in plate "Richard Ranft/1901," lr in pencil "Richard Ranft/Épreuve d'artiste," lr monogram M.N.
Bibliothèque Nationale, D. 3302; Ca 1c (xxe s.) Ranft.

Benjamin Jean Pierre Henri RIVIÈRE (1864-1951)

Rivière was an active participant in the artistic and literary environment of Le Chat Noir cabaret (1882-97) from the early 1880s and created several plays for Le Chat Noir's shadow theater, which he developed with Henry Somm. He is best known for his numerous series of color woodblock and color lithographic prints depicting views of Brittany and Paris; his first work in both media occurred in 1889 but, by that time, he had already produced at least five etchings printed in blue or purple and stamped in red with his distinctive Japanese-inspired monogram. Around 1889 both Rivière (in woodblock and lithography) and Cassatt (in etching) were beginning to experiment with color printmaking techniques, but the common impetus was the ukiyo-e Japanese print.
P. D. C.

[Armond Fields, Henri Rivière (Salt Lake City: Gibbs M. Smith, Inc., 1983)].

| 159 | Les Ébihiens, 1884

Etching in blue, 15.2 x 20.3 cm
Signed: lr artist's monogram
Zimmerli Art Museum, gift of Sara and Armond Fields.

| 160 | House on the Edge of the Water

Maison au bord de l'eau, 1884
Etching and aquatint in blue, 13.9 x 19.4 cm
Signed: ll artist's monogram "H.R.," lr monogram M.N.
Bibliothèque Nationale, D. 3302 (Musée du Luxembourg, 2 April 1931); Dc 422, t. VI.

| 161 | The Guillotine

La Guillotine, 1885
Etching in purple, 21 x 13.4 cm
Signed: ll in plate "Henri Rivière"
Bibliothèque Nationale, D. 11663 (G.-H. Rivière, 1 December 1959); Dc 422, t. VI.

Emmanuel (known as Manuel) ROBBE (1872-1936)

Pupil of the Académie Julian and then the École des Beaux Arts, Manuel Robbe first worked in lithography, creating color posters influenced by Art Nouveau (The Star, 1895). Thanks to Eugène Delâtre he soon discovered etching. Encouraged by Jacques Villon, and supported from 1898 by the publisher and dealer Edmond Sagot, Robbe became one of the leaders of the color etching movement: he worked with aquatint on zinc and printed his work à la poupée. His first works were printed by Delâtre, but Robbe soon began to print himself. An excellent technician, he placed velvety blacks against creamy whites, pale grays, misty pinks—or more unusual colors, browns, ochres, or bronze-greens. His favorite theme was women of the Belle Époque either performing their daily routine (The Toilette, Woman on a Chaise Longue, The Dressing Table, Maternal Quietude) or occupied in a more worldly setting (Tea, Choosing the Proof, Tricycle in the Wood). But he also depicted country scenes (The Harvesters), picturesque Paris (Place Clichy, The Chestnut Seller), or genre scenes and landscapes (Breton Market, Cockle Fishermen). His main publisher was Sagot, but in September-October 1898 Kleinmann sold Model's Rest (edition of forty, 20 francs). He was also published by Pierrefort, Gilquin, and Petit: Petit's 1911 catalogue included twenty-seven etchings, generally in editions of 200 and priced at 40 to 80 francs. At the Salon of the Société Nationale des Beaux-Arts in 1899 he exhibited two color etchings, The Swing and The Print Enthusiast; he exhibited again in 1901 (The Menders, The Flirt), in 1902 (Picnic published by Pierrefort, The Woman Reading with a Plaster Cast published by Sagot), in 1903 (Woman with Print and The Last Novel), and in 1904 (Nocturne and The Market, both published by Pierrefort). Manuel Robbe received a gold medal for etching at the Universal Exhibition in 1900 and participated in the Salon of the Société de la Gravure Originale en Couleurs. He became a member at its foundation in 1904 and exhibited Claudine (edition of sixty-five, 25 francs) in the first Salon. Robbe achieved success early in his career but fell into oblivion after 1930. He was on the fringe of artistic currents and tried to develop his printshop after World War I, working with artists such as Louis Icart, but his oeuvre did not return

to public favor until the late 1970s. M. G.
[Ch. Pérussaux, I. Kirschen, *Catalogue de l'exposition de la galerie Merill Chase* (Chicago, 1979-80); Ch. Pérussaux, "Manuel Robbe (1872-1936): gravures non-décrites," *La Revue de la Bibliothèque nationale* (September and December 1981, March and June 1982)]

162 *Choosing the Proof*
Le Choix de l'épreuve, 1900 (PK 107)
Sugarlift aquatint, 43.2 x 30.6 cm
Signed: lc in ink "Robbe—Le Choix de l'épreuve/tirée à 50 épreuves/Imprimerie Delâtre," Sagot monogram of 3 January 1900
Bibliothèque Nationale, D.L. 1900—125; AA3 Robbe.

163 *Woman on a Chaise Longue*
La Femme à la chaise longue, 1901 (P 12)
Drypoint and sugarlift aquatint, 31.8 x 38.8 cm
Signed: ll in pencil "Manuel Robbe," lr in pencil "Manuel Robbe/La Femme à la chaise longue"
Bibliothèque Nationale, D. 9631; AA3 Robbe.

164 *The Orchard—Houdelaincourt*
Le Verger—Houdelaincourt, c. 1903 (P 18)
*Aquatint and monotype, 30.4 x 39.7 cm
Signed: lr in pencil "Manuel Robbe/Le verger—Houdelaincourt"
Zimmerli Art Museum, David A. and Mildred H. Morse Art Acquisition Fund.

165 *Claudine*, 1903 (P 21)
*Etching and aquatint, 30.6 x 25 cm
Signed: lr in pencil "Manuel Robbe," ll in pencil "41/65"
Zimmerli Art Museum, David A. and Mildred H. Morse Art Acquisition Fund.

166 *The Harvesters*
Les Moissonneurs, n.d. (PK 161)
Sugarlift aquatint, roulette, and scraper, 37.9 x 40 cm
Signed: lr in pencil "Manuel Robbe/Les Moissonneurs"
Bibliothèque Nationale, D. 9631 (M. Pierrefort, 18 February 1901); AA3 Robbe.

167 *The Love Letter*
Le Billet doux, n.d. (PK 104)
Etching and aquatint, 32.9 x 23.4 cm
Signed: lr in pencil "Manuel Robbe/Le 'Billet Doux'"
Bibliothèque Nationale, D. 9631; AA3 Robbe.

168 *Spring*
Le Printemps, n.d.
Etching and aquatint, 49.2 x 34.6 cm
Signed: lr in pencil "Manuel Robbe/Le Printemps"
Bibliothèque Nationale, D. 9631; AA3 Robbe.

Théodore ROUSSEL (1847-1926)

Born in Lorient, Théodore Roussel moved to England in 1874 to pursue a career in art, but maintained his links with Paris, the capital of color etching. In 1885 he met James McNeill Whistler and, under his influence, etched some small drypoint portraits and views of Chelsea between the years 1887 and 1890. Like Whistler, Roussel launched into lithographic transfer at the beginning of the 1890s. But his greatest triumph remains his series of etchings, aquatints and softgrounds

in color, presented in mounts or frames also etched in color and designed to match the central print. The result of almost ten years' effort, *The Sea at Bognor, Summer, Anemones, China, Chelsea Palaces, The Thames, Evening, Last Poppies, Glowing Embers*, and *A Window Seen through a Window*, with their frames, often had to be passed more than twenty-four times through the press. In July 1899, the Goupil gallery exhibited the series for the first time. In 1904, Roussel participated in the first Salon of the Société de la Gravure Originale en Couleurs with *Anemones, China* and *Summer* (editions of sixty-five, 225, 575, and 475 francs respectively). President of the English Society of Color Etchers, which was founded in 1909, Roussel presented his series for a second time, along with five proofs and their frames, when he and other members exhibited at the Manzi-Joyant gallery in November-December 1910. M. G.
[Margaret Dunwoody Hausberg, *The Prints of Théodore Roussel, A Catalogue Raisonné* (New York, 1991)]

169 *Summer*
L'Été, c. 1890-1900 (H 143)
Etching and aquatint, 16.7 x 12.1 cm
Zimmerli Art Museum, David A. and Mildred H. Morse Art Acquisition Fund.

170 *Chelsea Palaces*
Les Palais de Chelsea, c. 1890-97 (H 144)
Etching and aquatint, 8.7 x 13.1 cm
Zimmerli Art Museum, David A. and Mildred H. Morse Art Acquisition Fund.

171 *Glowing Embers*
Lueur de tisons, c. 1890-97 (H 146)
Etching and aquatint, 24.4 x 20.5 cm
Signed: ll in plate
Zimmerli Art Museum, David A. and Mildred H. Morse Art Acquisition Fund.

172 *The Sea at Bognor*
La Mer à Bognor, 1895 (H 147)
Etching, drypoint, and softground, 27.3 x 30.5 cm
Zimmerli Art Museum, David A. and Mildred H. Morse Art Acquisition Fund.

173 *China*
La Chine, 1896-97 (H 148)
Etching, aquatint, and softground, 37.2 x 27.9 cm
Zimmerli Art Museum, David A. and Mildred H. Morse Art Acquisition Fund.

174 *Anemones*
Anémones, 1897 (H 149)
Etching and aquatint, 11.3 x 7.4 cm
Signed: lr in plate
Zimmerli Art Museum, David A. and Mildred H. Morse Art Acquisition Fund.

175 *Last Poppies*
Les Derniers Pavots, c. 1897 (H 150)
Etching and softground, 7.7 x 6.7 cm
Signed: lr in plate
Zimmerli Art Museum, David A. and Mildred H. Morse Art Acquisition Fund.

176 *The Thames, Evening*
La Tamise, le soir, c. 1897 (H 151)

Drypoint and aquatint, 6.8 x 12.1 cm
Signed: ll in plate
Zimmerli Art Museum, David A. and Mildred H. Morse Art Acquisition Fund.

177 *A Window Seen through a Window*
Une fenêtre vue à travers une fenêtre, c. 1897 (H 152)
Etching and aquatint, 22 x 14.2 cm
Signed: lc in plate
Zimmerli Art Museum, David A. and Mildred H. Morse Art Acquisition Fund.

Paul SIGNAC (1863-1935)

Primarily a painter, Paul Signac produced few engravings: approximately twenty lithographs, seven woodcuts, and seven etchings. However, from his first color print, *The Application of M. Charles Henry's Chromatic Circle* (1888), which preceded initial attempts in color by Bonnard and Lautrec, he applied the scientific theories of Divisionism that he later defined in his treatise D'*Eugène Delacroix au néo-impressionisme*, published in 1899. He kept his colors apart, attempting to depict all the nuances of light in his seascapes. He followed the same principle in his seven etchings. *Flessingue* (c. 1894) is printed in blue, its delicate variations in tone giving the impression of mist. The Bibliothèque Nationale's print is dedicated to Eugène Delâtre, which makes one think that Signac must have printed his rare intaglio etchings with Delâtre. M. G.
[E. W. Kornfeld and P. A. Wick, *Catalogue raisonné de l'œuvre gravé et lithographié de Paul Signac* (Bern, 1974)]

178a *Flessingue*, c. 1894 (KW 7)
Etching in blue, 17.7 x 22.3 cm
Signed: lr in pencil "à Eug. Delâtre/en reconnaissance et en toute sympathie/P. Signac"
Bibliothèque Nationale, D. 7374 (legs A. Curtis, 26 October 1949, no.4517); AA3 Signac.

178b *Flessingue*, c. 1894 (KW 7)
Etching in blue and gray, 18 x 22.5 cm
Signed: lr in pencil "tiré à 15 épreuves, no. 12, P. Signac"
Zimmerli Art Museum, Mindy and Ramon Tublitz Purchase Fund.

Maurice SIMONET

We have no information on this artist.

179 *Autumn Morning*
Matinée d'Automne, c. 1900
*Aquatint, 38 x 34.9 cm
Signed: lr in pencil "Maurice Simonet"
Zimmerli Art Museum, David A. and Mildred H. Morse Art Acquisition Fund.

Théophile-Alexandre STEINLEN (1859-1923)

Arriving in Paris from Switzerland in 1879, Steinlen's social conscience was raised by reading Émile Zola's novel of urban poverty, *L'Assommoir*, and this was to play a significant role in his art. By 1883, Steinlen had also become an active participant in the literary-artistic milieu of Le Chat Noir cabaret in Montmartre, which served as an important catalyst for his prolific career as a printmaker, poster artist, and illustrator of journals and books. In 1898, under the instruction of

Eugène Delâtre, Steinlen began creating black-and-white and color etchings, usually in quite small editions. In *Prostitute and Pimp*, two figures emerge from the darkness of the rich aquatint ground colored *à la poupée*; working from dark to light, as in a mezzotint, and burnishing away the ink-receiving surface, Steinlen modeled and silhouetted the figures. *The Washerwomen*, printed from three plates, portrays a working-class theme common in his art. Steinlen's socially oriented subject matter and innovative manipulation of color intaglio techniques, *à la poupée* and *au repérage*, had great influence on artists such as Sunyer, Bottini, Villon, and Picasso. P. D. C.

[Ernest de Crauzat, *L'Œuvre gravé et lithographié de Steinlen* (Paris: Société de Propagation des Livres d'Art, 1913)]

180   *The Washerwomen*
Les Blanchisseuses, 1898 (C 22—III)
Etching and aquatint, 36 x 26.9 cm
Bibliothèque Nationale, D. 7374 (legs A. Curtis, 26 October 1949, no.4636); Dc 385, t. I.

181   *Prostitute and Pimp*
Fille et souteneur, 1898 (C 23)
Etching and aquatint, 24 x 12.2 cm
Signed: lr in pencil "Steinlen"
Zimmerli Art Museum, David A. and Mildred H. Morse Art Acquisition Fund.

182   *Parasol*
Ombrelle, 1898 (C 24)
Etching, drypoint, and aquatint, 23.8 x 12.2 cm
Signed: lr in red crayon "Steinlen"
Bibliothèque Nationale, D. 8207 (Mme de Crauzat, 30 January 1952); Dc 385, t. I.

183a   *Reclining Nude*
Nu couché, 1898 (C 26—I)
Etching, drypoint, and aquatint, 19 x 29.2 cm
Signed: lr in red crayon "Steinlen"
Bibliothèque Nationale, Dc 385, t. I.

183b   *Reclining Nude*
Nu couché, 1898 (C 26—II)
Etching, drypoint, and aquatint, 19.5 x 30 cm
Signed: lr in red crayon "Steinlen"
Bibliothèque Nationale, D. 7374 (legs A. Curtis, 26 October 1949, no. 4648); Dc 385, t. I.

184   *Little Cat*
Petit Chat, 1898 (C 27—III)
Drypoint and roulette, 10 x 16.7 cm
Signed: ur in image "A l'ami Eug. Delâtre/Ce premier cuivre—résultat de ses/bons conseils et de la gentillesse de/son petit chat—est dédié/juin 98/Steinlen"
Bibliothèque Nationale, D. 8207; Dc 385, t. I.

185   *The House on the Edge of the Village*
La Maison à l'entrée du village, 1902 (C 68—final state)
Softground, aquatint, and drypoint, 18.8 x 30.6 cm
Signed: lr in pencil "Steinlen," lr in pencil "Planches reprises—état définitif. No. 9"
Bibliothèque Nationale, D. 8207; Dc 385, t. I.

Joachim SUNYER Y MIRO (1875-1956)
Sunyer lived in Montmartre from 1894 to 1911 and then returned to Spain. By 1897 his art, as represented by the series of eight color lithographs for Jehan Rictus's *Les Soliloques du pauvre*, was closely related in style and social content to that of Steinlen. Steinlen began creating color etchings with Eugène Delâtre in 1898 and may well have introduced Sunyer to him. Sunyer acted as an important link between the Montmartre avant-garde and Spanish newcomers such as Iturrino and Picasso. In 1901 Sunyer moved to the complex of artists' studios later known as the Bateau-Lavoir, where Picasso also lived from 1904 to 1909. P. D. C.

186   *Shoelace Seller*
Le Marchand de lacets, 1899
Etching and aquatint, 24 x 18.8 cm
Signed: lr in plate "Sunyer/99," lr in pencil "Sunyer," "Sunyer/Le Marchand de lacets"
Bibliothèque Nationale, D. 9633 (M. Pierrefort, 18 February 1901); Bf 22 (xxe s.) Sunyer.

187   *The Ragpicker*
Le Chiffonnier, 1900 (final state)
Etching, 24 x 17.5 cm
Signed: ll in plate "Sunyer/1900," lr in pencil "Sunyer/Le Chiffonnier"
Bibliothèque Nationale, D. 9633; Bf 22 (20th c.) Sunyer.

188   *Secrets*
Confidences, c. 1900
*Etching, aquatint, and monotype, 18.5 x 20.5 cm
Signed: lr in pencil "Sunyer"
Zimmerli Art Museum, David A. and Mildred H. Morse Art Acquisition Fund.

189   *Students in the Luxembourg Gardens*
La Grande Allée du Luxembourg ou Étudiants au jardin du Luxembourg, c. 1900
*Etching, drypoint, and aquatint, 45 x 31.9 cm
Signed: lr in pencil "Sunyer"
Zimmerli Art Museum, Joyce and Alvin Glasgold Purchase Fund.

190   *At the Luxembourg Gardens*
Au Luxembourg, c. 1900
Etching and aquatint, 26.9 x 37.7 cm
Signed: lr in pencil "Sunyer," "Sunyer/Au Luxembourg"
Bibliothèque Nationale, D. 9633; Bf 22 (20th c.) Sunyer.

191   *Marcel Legay*, c. 1900
*Etching and aquatint touched with pigment, 32.4 x 24.9 cm
Signed: lr in pencil "15/30/Sunyer"
Zimmerli Art Museum, Class of 1944 Purchase Fund.

192   *At the Puppet Show*
Devant Guignol, c. 1900
Etching and aquatint, 22.3 x 31.3 cm
Signed: lr in pencil "Sunyer," "Sunyer/Devant Guignol"
Bibliothèque Nationale, D. 9633; Bf 22 (20th c.) Sunyer.

Maurice-Charles-Louis TAQUOY (1878-1952)
Born at Mareuil-sur-Ay (Marne), Maurice Taquoy was a pupil of Baschet and Schommer at the Académie Julian. The founding secretary of the Salon d'Automne in 1903, he exhibited there from 1904 and at the Indépendants from 1905. He contributed to *La Vie Parisienne* from 1906 to 1911. Specializing in racing scenes, he participated in the 1904 Salon de la Gravure Originale en Couleurs with six color etchings in editions of fifteen to fifty. He was present each year (except 1908) until 1913. Georges Petit's 1911 catalogue includes four of his prints, *Returning to the Kennels*, *The Kill*, *Animals Together*, and *The Huntsmen's Dinner* (editions of 200, 40 francs), an indication of his commercial success. M. G.

193   *Ed. Sagot*, 1906
Aquatint, 16.4 x 16.3 cm
Signed: ll in plate in reverse "M. Taquoy 06"
Zimmerli Art Museum.

194   *Two Hounds*
Deux Chiens Courants, 1906
Etching and aquatint, 28 x 39.7 cm
Signed: lr in plate "06 Maurice Taquoy," lr in pencil "Maurice Taquoy 06," ll in pencil "no. 36"
Zimmerli Art Museum, gift of Mr. and Mrs. Herbert Littman.

195   *Two Pointers*
Deux Pointers, 1907
Etching and aquatint, 24.7 x 45.6 cm
Signed: ll in plate "Maurice Taquoy 07," lr in pencil "Maurice Taquoy 07," ll in pencil "no. 15"
Zimmerli Art Museum, gift of Mr. and Mrs. Herbert Littman.

Frits THAULOW (1847-1906)
Born in Norway, Thaulow arrived in Paris in 1874 and spent most of the rest of his life in France. Sympathetic to the modernist tendencies of the Impressionists, he was primarily a landscape painter. *The Sentinel*, published by Georges Petit, was exhibited at the 1903 Salon of the Société Nationale des Beaux-Arts. Thaulow's color etchings fall into the category of reproductive printmaking: they are based on original designs by the artist, but he did not create the intaglio plates himself. They are some of the more aesthetically successful examples of the very finished, representational works promoted by prominent turn-of-the-century galleries to a middle-class audience that was receptive to relatively inexpensive color prints based upon work by popular and established artists. P. D. C.

196   *The Sentinel*
La Sentinelle, 1903
Etching and aquatint touched with watercolor, 59 x 47 cm
Signed: lr in pencil "Frits Thaulow," ll monogram "Georges Petit Paris"
Zimmerli Art Museum.

Abel TRUCHET (1857-1918)
Truchet studied at the Académie Julian. A humorist, illustrator, and printmaker, he participated in the 1883 exhibition of the Société des Arts Incohérents and later became a founding member of the Société des Humoristes. He was closely involved in the artistic-literary cabaret life of Montmartre

and, in particular, the Quat'-z-Arts cabaret (founded in 1893) for which he served as artist-in-residence by creating its 1894 poster, interior decorations, and illustrations for the *Journal des Quat'-z-Arts* (1897-98). In 1907 Truchet exhibited at the Salon of the Société de la Gravure Originale en Couleurs; his work in color etching apparently dates from around this time. However he is better known for his work in color lithography, such as his large lithographs of c. 1902 depicting dancers at the Moulin Rouge. P. D. C.

| 197 | *Parisian Woman*
La Parisienne, c. 1900
Etching and aquatint, 42 x 33.2 cm
Signed: ll in plate "Abel Truchet"
Zimmerli Art Museum, gift of Mr. and Mrs. Herbert Littman

Jacques VILLON (also known as **Gaston DUCHAMP**) (1875-1963)
Jacques Villon arrived in Paris in 1895 and became a pupil at Cormon's studio. In 1899 his friend Francis Jourdain, who with Eugène Delâtre introduced him to the technique, encouraged him to produce his first color etchings. Probably printed by Eugène Delâtre, they were published by Edmond Sagot, who remained Villon's principal publisher until 1911. After this brief period, Villon abandoned aquatint and dedicated himself to black-and-white intaglio printing. It seems that his interest in color etching faded from about 1906: while he exhibited at the Salons of 1901 (*Sulking, Hey, Class*), 1902 (*Bibi la Purée, Little Mother*), and, most importantly, at the first Salon of the Société de la Gravure Originale en Couleurs in 1904 (he was one of the main exhibitors, showing seventeen works), he showed only four works at the 1905 Salon de la Gravure Originale en Couleurs (*Under the Tent, Farm at Bendelière, Horses of the Wood, Chaise Longue*), and did not participate thereafter. His period of production was short but intense. Although his work features the usual turn-of-the-century themes of Parisian and military life, it is striking because of the power of its construction and its color: the wide planes of red and yellow in *The Cards*, the acid-green of *Cakewalk*, and the stylization of *The Abductor* have enormous strength, and yet other works, such as *Reading* (1901), display a subtle combination of etched lines highlighted by aquatint colors. His relatively small editions, usually of fifty—except for *The Cards, The Abductor* and *Lady in Blue* (twenty-five) and *Under the Tent* (seventy-five)—show that Villon envisaged color etching as an original graphic experience rather than as a commercial enterprise. M. G.
[Jacqueline Auberty and Charles Pérussaux, *Jacques Villon, Catalogue de son œuvre gravé* (Paris: P/ Prouté, 1950)]
[Colette de Ginestet and Catherine Pouillon, *Jacques Villon, les estampes et les illustrations* (Paris: Arts et Métiers graphiques, 1979)]

| 198 | *Negro Made Good*
Le Nègre en bonne fortune, 1899 (AP 4; GP E22)
*Etching and aquatint, 25.5 x 33.4 cm
Signed: ur in plate "Jacques Villon/99," lr in black crayon "Jacques Villon 19/25"
Bibliothèque Nationale, D. 3302 (Musée du Luxembourg, 2 April 1931); Ef 437, t. I.

| 199 | *Spanish Dancer*
Danseuse espagnole, 1899 (AP 5; GP E23)
*Drypoint and aquatint, 50.4 x 35.6 cm
Signed: ll in plate "Jacques Villon/99," lr in pencil "Jacques Villon 25/25"
Bibliothèque Nationale, A. 10622 (Jacques Villon, 30 January 1950); Ef 437, t. I.

| 200 | *Mlle. Ellen Andrée*
Mlle. Ellen Andrée, 1900 (AP 24; GP E 39)
Etching and aquatint, 35.6 x 28.5 cm
Signed: lr in pencil "Jacques Villon 2/30," ll in plate "Villon"
Zimmerli Art Museum, David A. and Mildred H. Morse Art Acquisition Fund.

| 201 | *Sulking*
La Boudeuse, 1900 (AP 18; GP E 37)
*Etching and aquatint, 17.7 x 28.3 cm
Signed: c in plate "Jacques Villon/00," ll in pencil "Boudeuse," lr in pencil "Jacques Villon"
Bibliothèque Nationale, D. 1218 (Jacques Villon, 10 May 1912); Ef 437, t. I.

| 202a | *On a Bench*
Sur un banc, 1900 (AP 16; GP E 38)
Etching, drypoint, and aquatint, 33.9 x 26.8 cm
Signed: in plate "Jacques Villon/00," lr monogram M.N.
Bibliothèque Nationale, D. 3302 (Musée du Luxembourg, 2 April 1931); Ef 437, t. I.

| 202b | *On a Bench*
Sur un banc, 1900 (AP 16; GP E 38)
Etching, drypoint, and aquatint, 33.8 x 26.7 cm
Signed: in plate "Jacques Villon/00," lr "Jacques Villon/3/30"
Bibliothèque Nationale, D. 1218; Ef 437, t. I.

| 203 | *Life Is Not a Novel*
La Vie n'est pas un roman, 1900 (AP 21; GP E 43)
*Etching, drypoint and aquatint, 29.7 x 22.8 cm
Signed: lr in plate "Jacques Villon/00/La Vie n'est pas un roman/Alphonse Daudet—Jack," lr "A. Delâtre/Jacques Villon/00"
Bibliothèque Nationale, A. 14384; Ef 437, t. I.

| 204 | *Father Noret Killing a Cockerel*
Le Père Noret tuant un coq, 1900 (AP 23; GP E47)
Sugarlift aquatint on sulfurized brown parchment, 21.3 x 13.2 cm
Signed: ll in pencil "Jacques Villon"
Bibliothèque Nationale, D. 1976—4134 (Mme Marcel Duchamp, 26 July 1976); Ef 437, t. I.

| 205 | *Society Comedy*
Comédie de société, 1903 (AP 43; GP E75)
Etching and aquatint, 50 x 42 cm
Signed: ll in pencil "Comédie de société," lr in pencil "Jacques Villon"
Bibliothèque Nationale, D. 1218 (Jacques Villon, 10 May 1912); Ef 437, t. I.

| 206 | *The Cards*
Les Cartes, 1903 (AP 44; GP E76)
Etching and aquatint, 35 x 44.7 cm
Signed: lr in plate "Jacques Villon/03," ll in pencil "Les cartes," lr in brown crayon "Jacques Villon"
Bibliothèque Nationale, D. 1218 (Jacques Villon, 10 May 1912); Ef 437, t. I.

| 207 | *Women of Ouessant*
Les Femmes d'Ouessant, 1904 (AP 63; GP E 81)
Etching, drypoint, roulette, and aquatint, 27.4 x 37.9 cm
Signed: ll in pencil "Épreuve d'artiste," lr in pencil "Jacques Villon," lr "Les Femmes d'Ouessant"
Bibliothèque Nationale, D. 1218 (Jacques Villon, 10 May 1912); Ef 437, t. I.

| 208 | *Cakewalk*, 1904 (AP 56—I; GP E102)
Etching and aquatint, 30.5 x 42.2 cm
Signed: ll in pencil "Épreuve d'artiste," lr "Jacques Villon"
Bibliothèque Nationale, A. 1988—74500; Ef 437, t. I.

Bibliography

ALEXANDRE, Arsène, *Jean-François Raffaëlli, peintre, graveur et sculpteur*, Paris, 1909.

AUBERTY, Jacqueline, and PÉRUSSAUX, Charles, *Jacques Villon, catalogue de son œuvre gravé*, Paris, P. Prouté, 1950.

BAILLY-HERZBERG, Janine, *Correspondance de Camille Pissarro*, vol. I 1865-1885; vol. II 1886-1890; vol. III 1891-1894; vol. IV 1895-1898, Paris, 1980-1988.

BAILLY-HERZBERG, Janine, *Dictionnaire de l'estampe en France, 1830-1950*, Paris, Arts et Métiers graphiques, 1985.

BÉRALDI, Henri, *Graveurs du XIXe siècle*, vol. III, Paris, 1885.

BERTIN, Claudie, *Henri Guérard (1846-1897), l'œuvre gravé*, 3 vol., thesis from the Ecole du Louvre, Paris, 1975.

BOURCARD, Gustave, *Félix Buhot: catalogue descriptif de son œuvre gravé*, 1899; ed. revised by James Goodfriends, New York, Martin Gordon, Inc., 1979.

BOYER, Patricia Eckert, and CATE, Phillip Dennis, *L'Estampe originale, Artistic Printmaking in France 1893-95*, Amsterdam, Vincent Van Gogh Museum, 1991.

BOYER, Patricia Eckert, and CATE, Phillip Dennis, *The Circle of Toulouse-Lautrec: An Exhibition of Work of the Artist and his Close Associates*, New Brunswick, The Jane Voorhees Zimmerli Art Museum, 1985.

BREESKIN, Adelyn D., *The Graphic Work of Mary Cassatt, A Catalogue raisonné*, New York, H. Bittner and Co., 1948.

BURCH, R.M., *Colour Printing and Colour Printers*, with a chapter on the new techniques by W. Gamble, Edinburgh, Paul Harris Publishing, 1983.

CARIOU, A., *Charles Cottet et la Bretagne*, Raillé, Ursa-Le Chasse-Marée, 1988.

Catalogue des archives de la maison Gustave Pellet—Maurice Exsteens, Bern, Klipstein and Kornfeld, 1962.

CATE, Phillip Dennis, *Charles Maurin (1856-1914)*, New York, Lucien Goldschmidt, 1978.

CATE, Phillip Dennis, *Seeking the Floating World: The Japanese Spirit in Turn-of-the-Century France*, Tokyo, 1989.

CATE, Phillip Dennis, *The Graphic Arts and French Society, 1871-1914*, New Brunswick, Rutgers University Press, 1988.

CATE, Phillip Dennis, and HITCHINGS, Sinclair Hamilton, *The Color Revolution, Color Lithography in France, 1890-1900*, New Brunswick, The Rutgers University Art Gallery, 1978.

CRAUZAT, Ernest DE, *L'Œuvre gravé et lithographié de Steinlen*, Paris, Société de propagation des livres d'art, 1913.

DELTEIL, Loÿs, *Le Peintre-Graveur illustré*, vol. XVI-XVII, Paris, 1923.

FIELDS, Armond, *Henri Rivière*, Salt Lake City, Gibbs M. Smith Inc., 1983.

FRÉCHURET, Maurice, *L'Œuvre de Charles Maurin. Un symbolisme du réel*, Doctoral thesis in History of Art, Université de Lyon II, 1986, 4 vol.

GATIER, Félix, *Catalogue de l'œuvre gravé de Pierre Gatier*, to appear in *Nouvelles de l'estampe*.

GATIER, Félix, "Pierre Gatier," *Nouvelles de l'estampe*, no. 27, May-June 1976.

GATIER, Pierre, *Traité de l'aquatinte en trois couleurs*, unedited manuscript, Toulon, 1910, Paris, 1919, Isle-Adam, 1920.

GEISER, Bernhard., *Picasso, peintre-graveur: catalogue illustré de l'œuvre gravé et lithographié, 1899-1931*, Bern, 1933, 2nd ed., 1955.

GINESTET, Colette DE, and POUILLON, Catherine, *Jacques Villon, les estampes et les illustrations*, Paris, Arts et Métiers graphiques, 1979.

GUILLEMOT, Maurice, *Georges Jeanniot, peintre-graveur*, Paris, Maison du Livre, 1901.

HAUSBERG, Margaret Dunwoody, *The Prints of Theodore Roussel, A Catalogue Raisonné*, New York, 1991.

IVES, Colta Feller, *The Great Wave: The Influence of Japanese Woodcuts on French Prints*, New York, Metropolitan Museum of Art, 1974.

JANIN, Clément, *Verzeichniss der graphische Arbeiter Charles Cottet. Die Graphischen Künste*, Vienna, 1909, vol. 32, p. 49-54.

KORNFELD, E.W. and WICK, P.A., *Catalogue raisonné de l'œuvre gravé et lithographié de Paul Signac*, Bern, 1974.

E.S. Krouglicoff, Life and Work, Leningrad, P.E. Korniloff, 1969, in Russian.

LARAN, Jean, *L'Œuvre gravé d'Eugène Béjot*, Paris, 1937.

LEROY-CRÈVECŒUR, Marie, *La Vie parisienne en 1900 à travers l'estampe en couleurs*, exhib. cat., Osaka-Tokyo, 1991.

LEYMARIE, Jean and MELOT, Michel, *Les Gravures des impressionnistes Manet, Pissarro, Renoir, Cézanne, Sisley*, Paris, 1971.

LISTER, Raymond, *Prints and Printmaking. A Dictionnary and Handbook of the Art in Nineteenth Century Britain*, London, Methuen, 1984.

LOTZ-BRISSONNEAU, A., *L'Œuvre gravé d'Auguste Lepère*, Paris, 1905.

LOUVET-BIROT, Jacqueline, *Vie, œuvre et art du peintre Bernard Boutet de Monvel (1884-1949)*, Master's thesis in Art and Archeology, Paris-IV—Sorbonne, 1979.

MARCHESSEAU, Daniel, *Catalogue raisonné de l'œuvre gravé de Marie Laurencin*, Tokyo, 1981.

MATHEWS, Nancy Mowll, *Cassatt and her Circle. Selected Letters*, New York, Abbeville Press, 1984.

MATHEWS, Nancy Mowll, and SHAPIRO, Barbara Stern, *Mary Cassatt: The Color Prints*, New York, Abrams, 1989.

MAYOR, A. Hyatt, *Prints and People, a Social History of Printed Pictures*, New York, 1971.

MORANE, Daniel, *Maxime Maufra 1861-1918. Catalogue raisonné de l'œuvre gravé*, Musée de Pont-Aven, 1986.

MOUREY, Gabriel, "Coloured Etchings in France," *The Studio*, vol. XXII, no. 95, February 1901, pp. 3-14 and 94-103.

PENNELL, Joseph, *Etchers and Etching*, New York, The Macmillan Company, 1936.

PÉRUSSAUX, Charles, "Manuel Robbe (1872-1936): gravures non décrites," *La Revue de la Bibliothèque nationale*, September and December 1981, March and June 1982.

PORTALIS, Roger, "La gravure en couleurs," *La Gazette des Beaux-Arts*, February 1890.

PUGET, Catherine, *Victor-Joseph Roux-Champion, 1871-1953*, exhib. cat., Musée de Pont-Aven, 1991.

RAFFAELLI, Jean-François, *Préface du catalogue du 10e Salon de la gravure originale en couleurs*, November 1913, Paris, G. Petit, 1913.

RAMIRO, Erastène, *Catalogue de l'œuvre gravé de Louis Legrand*, Paris, 1896.

RIOTOR, Léon, "Les eaux-fortes en couleurs à la galerie Georges Petit," *L'Art décoratif*, February 1905.

ROGER-MILES, L., *Louis Legrand, peintre, graveur, illustrateur*, Paris, printed for Charles Meunier, 1902.

SOUTHARD, Edna Carter, *Georges Bottini: Painter of Montmartre. Essay and Catalogue*, Oxford, Ohio, Miami University Art Museum, 1984.

TABANELLI, R., *Edgar Chahine, catalogue de l'œuvre gravé*, Milan, Il Mercante di Stampe, 1977.

UZANNE, Octave, "La gravure en couleurs. Le renouveau de la taille-douce polychrome," *Le Livre moderne*, no. 9, 10 September 1890.

WICHMANN, Siegfried, *Japonisme, The Japanese Influence on Western Art in the 19th and 20th Centuries*, New York, Harmony Books, 1981.

Index

Numbers in italics correspond to pages featuring illustrations.